MODELLING AND PAINTING
World War II US Figures
and Vehicles

70128 U.S.A.

MODELLING AND PAINTING
World War II US Figures and Vehicles

RAY HASKINS

THE CROWOOD PRESS

First published in 2020 by
The Crowood Press Ltd
Ramsbury, Marlborough
Wiltshire SN8 2HR

enquiries@crowood.com

www.crowood.com

British Library Cataloguing-in-Publication Data
A catalogue record for this book is available from the British Library.

ISBN 978 1 78500 715 6

Typeset by Shane O'Dwyer, Swindon, Wiltshire

Printed and bound in India by Replika Press Pvt Ltd

CONTENTS

	Acknowledgements	6
	Preface	7
	Introduction	9
CHAPTER 1	TOOLS AND MATERIALS	11
CHAPTER 2	THE PACIFIC, 1941–5	18
CHAPTER 3	NORTH AFRICA AND THE *TORCH* LANDINGS	42
CHAPTER 4	SICILY AND ITALY, 1943–5	59
CHAPTER 5	NORMANDY	69
CHAPTER 6	THE SEINE TO THE BULGE, 25 AUGUST 1944 – JANUARY 1945	85
CHAPTER 7	THE END OF THE WAR IN EUROPE, MARCH–MAY 1945	102
CHAPTER 8	WORKING WITH SOFT PLASTIC SOLDIERS AND BASING FIGURES	118
	Useful Contacts	123
	Bibliography	124
	Index	125

Acknowledgements

I WOULD LIKE TO thank a few people without whom I would not have been able to illustrate this book, or indeed experience building and painting such fine figures and models: Tony Barton, the designer of AB miniatures, Tom Walsh, owner of Milicast Models, Tony Chadburn of Raventhorpe Miniatures, who provided the 20mm figures used in two chapters, Mark Dixon of CP Models and TQD Castings and Matt Hingley of Elhiem Miniatures.

A special thank you goes to Owen Conner, the Uniforms and Heraldry Curator at the National Museum of the Marine Corps, Triangle, Virginia, who very kindly provided the pictures of museum artefacts that feature in Chapter 2. Owen was also kind enough to write the captions for those pictures as well, which describe them perfectly.

Preface

THE AIM OF THIS book is to bring the US Army of World War II to life on the gaming table as well as the display cabinet for both wargamer and collector alike. Practical step-by-step instructions demonstrate how to create realistic models in metal, resin and plastic, using various techniques from hand painting to airbrushing.

My modelling career started in the mid-1970s when, five years old and living in Enniskillen, Northern Ireland, I received my first Airfix kit. This sparked an interest that has grown and developed over the years, allowing me to graduate from modelling with plastic soldiers to modern metal versions. It has been a journey that could be rather trying at times, but mostly it has been engrossing and enjoyable.

I still have very fond memories of taking the weekly Saturday journey into town with my mother while she did her shopping, and waiting patiently until we could, at last, visit the local toyshop, which seemed to stock every Airfix kit available. After handing over my pocket money for the chosen kit, the journey home was filled with anticipation and excitement at the prospect of building my latest prize. At that time painting the models was optional, but the fun I had in building them was boundless.

Many years later, and a lot older, I am happy to say that I still feel that same excitement at the thought of tackling a new modelling subject, no matter what size: from a small kit with only a few parts to one with many hundreds. I am an avid modeller in 1:72 and 1:76 scales, Wargaming is a significant part of my modelling hobby and I enjoy every aspect, from researching a unit to using it on the tabletop battlefield.

Introduction

MODELLING IS A PERSONAL hobby: all modellers like to add their own mark or style to the work they do. Taking this into account, this book provides a guide to show how to achieve pleasing results. As such, the reader is encouraged to take what they need from it, and to add or adapt the techniques shown to their preferred way of doing things. Good modellers continually develop their practical skills and are not afraid to try new techniques. This is part of the joy of modelling.

Modelling products and materials have changed quite dramatically over the last ten years: there is now a wealth of products available that have changed the hobby for the better. It is now much easier for the newcomer to make a start in modelling with just a few select items that will enable a standard-built model to become unique and something to be proud of.

DO YOUR HOMEWORK

When thinking of modelling a tank that fought in Normandy in June 1944, for example, find out about:

- the units that operated it, their uniforms and their kit
- where they fought and against whom
- the time of year and/or the predominant weather conditions at that time
- the type of terrain/groundcover
- the markings it may have carried, such as the names painted on it by its crew

BACKGROUND RESEARCH

An important, and sometimes overlooked, aspect of modelling is research. This should be the cornerstone of any modelling project from the very beginning. 'What?', 'where?' and 'how?' are three questions that provide an important starting point and will help to steer further investigation. Background research at this stage could help to avoid a disastrous end result, so time spent checking up on details, via the internet or through relevant books or television programmes, is always time well spent.

During WWII the US armed forces standardized the equipment they used. The term 'GI', which is an abbreviation of Government Issue, arose and is still in use today to describe American soldiers during WWII. (By contrast, US soldiers in WWI were nicknamed 'doughboys'.) Every soldier, sailor and airman was issued with the same kit relevant to their role and location at that time during the war, from the Central Pacific to the freezing cold of the Belgian Ardennes. A paratrooper who landed in Normandy in June 1944 wore a different uniform to one who fought during Operation *Market Garden* in September 1944, just a few months later. The difference between the uniforms worn by the Marines who fought on Wake Island in 1941 and those who fought on Tarawa in 1944 is vast. The exception to this is the tank crews, who wore more or less the same uniform, with only minor variations, all through the war.

Then there are vehicle markings: the US Army did not always use a white star on their vehicles; in fact, in the early days of WWII they used a yellow star in North Africa.

Following on from the recommendation to undertake research, there is little point in writing this book without providing some historical context to the models. As such, this book is divided into several chapters, each covering a specific theatre of the war in which US forces were involved. Presented in chronological order, the chapters start in the Pacific from 1941 to 1945 and end in war-torn Germany in May 1945. Features specific to each campaign are modelled, such as the relevant uniforms and equipment, and the main supporting vehicles. Where models could potentially have been included in a number of chapters, they appear in the chapter covering the period during which they had the most impact: the models of tracked landing vehicles (LVT), for example, have been included in the Pacific chapter as they were first used in a combat role at the Battle of Tarawa in 1943 and prior to this they were only used to bring supplies from ship to shore. Similarly, although paratroopers were deployed in the Allied invasion of Sicily in 1943, it was in Normandy in 1944 where they had the most significant impact.

This book covers painting and modelling the service personnel of the United States of America, and also extends to the modelling of some of the combat vehicles they used, including the M4 Sherman tank and some of the various tank destroyers that were used from 1942 to 1945. Both vehicles and figures will be covered in 1:56, 1:72 and 1:76 scales.

Tools and Materials 1

BEFORE YOU BEGIN ANY modelling or painting project, it is important to ensure there is sufficient workspace and the work area is both well lit and comfortable. The lighting should be appropriate for both building kits and painting: using several easily positioned lamps, such as anglepoise, rather than overhead lighting is recommended.

Even with good positional lighting, small-scale modelling and the painting of fine details can take their toll on the eyes. A good solution is to use an opti-visor, available in various forms and prices. Looked after, this will be an invaluable investment.

A chair that provides adequate support to minimize slouching and prevent both neck and back pain is essential. The modeller may be engrossed in their work and sitting in the same position for many hours, so a chair that is both comfortable and practical is important and makes the process of modelling more enjoyable and less of a chore. Chairs designed for use in businesses can be bought from commercial office suppliers at reasonable prices.

Finally, the work area should be well organized with everything that is needed in easy reach: after all, spending time looking for something is time taken away from the fun part.

LIGHTBULBS

Warm white lightbulbs cast a light with a yellowish hue and this will affect the perception of any paint colours being used. Daylight bulbs are better as they cast a pure white light that makes it easier to see colours as well as details. They have a colour-rendering index (CRI), the measure of a light source's ability to render colours faithfully, of around 80 per cent. Full spectrum lightbulbs, which offer a light as close as possible to natural daylight, have a CRI of around 96 per cent, and are the best choice but they are more expensive.

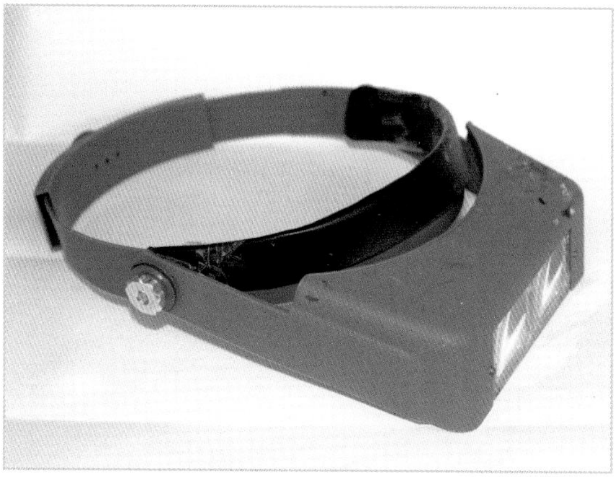

Optivisors come in several types, but they all perform the same task of magnification.

ESSENTIAL EQUIPMENT

Health and safety essentials

Safety cannot be overlooked. Eye protection is vital when cutting something that may, at any moment, fly into the air. Safety glasses do not cost much and so it might be worth having more than one pair to hand.

When using aerosols and airbrushing, or working with anything that creates dust, such as sanding, always wear a good quality mask. This should not be a dust mask but a proper respirator mask with filters, which can be purchased at any good high street DIY store. Dust masks are fine for keeping larger dust particles at bay, but when using an airbrush or aerosol with solvents or similar a good respirator is essential. Make sure that your work area is also well ventilated.

Cutting mat and tools

A good-sized cutting mat is important: it protects the surface underneath as well as prolonging the life of the blade being used. For any type of modelling you will need a few basic tools, starting with a good quality knife. Exacto make fine modelling knives and scalpels, and have a wide range of blades that are both very sharp and strong. A good set of small files is also needed; these are relatively inexpensive and can be found in most model shops as well as online. A couple of pairs of wire cutters are handy to have. These come in two sizes: the larger ones are suitable for cutting wire, for example, to make antennas for vehicles, and the smaller ones are good for removing large plastic parts from sprues. A set of tweezers is handy to have for lifting and positioning small parts, as well as the handling of other tricky jobs.

Power tools

A Dremel, or similar hand-held powered multitool, is highly recommended as it can be used for cutting, sanding, polishing and other tasks. With the circular cutting disc attached, it is possible to remove the finest details of a model without harming it. It is an investment purchase but will soon prove to be an invaluable tool.

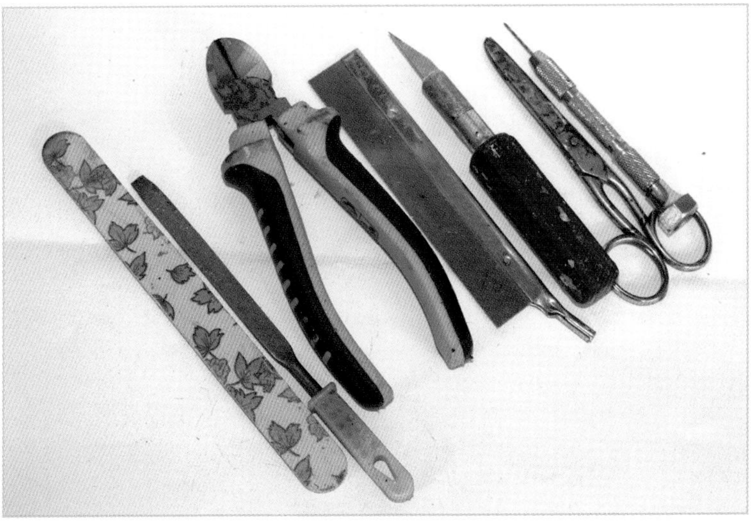

RIGHT: A small but useful selection of tools: files, scissors, an emery board and a craft knife with a handle that can also hold a razor saw blade.

BELOW: A Dremel hand-held cordless power tool. This two-speed model is capable of performing tasks that need precision, such as removing excess resin from models.

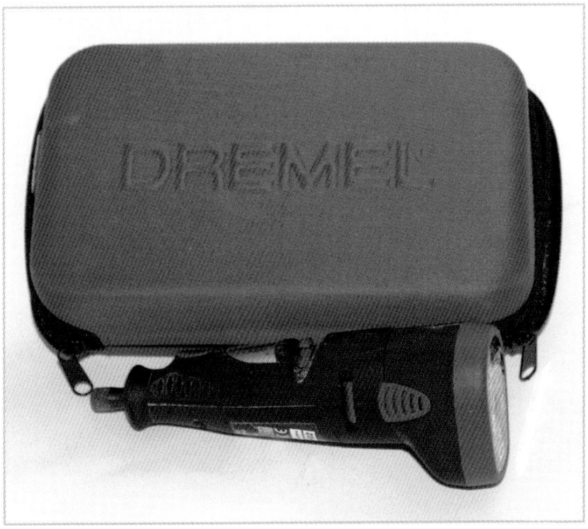

Plasticard

It is useful to have a selection of different thicknesses of plasticard at hand. These can be used for basing and conversions, as well as for making items such as stowage boxes for vehicles. Wire, of various diameters, also has many uses, for example making antennas. Both plasticard and wire can be bought from local model shops or on-line.

Clamps and vice

A selection of clamps is useful for holding parts together while glue sets. A pin vice, available in various sizes, also comes in very handy when drilling out delicate areas such as hands on figures and gun barrels on vehicles. Because they are hand turned, as well as being very accurate, they do not create any heat and so will not melt plastic. They take a variety of drill bits designed for hobby use, from the finest to the largest, and the bonus is they are inexpensive.

Fillers and modelling putties

Miliput and Green Stuff are two-part putties that once mixed in the correct amounts (50-50) can be used for conversions, adding detail, filling gaps and making accessories such as bedrolls, blankets, sandbags, etc. Always have at least one of these products to hand – it will come in handy. They can be bought either on-line or from any good model shop. In addition, there are plastic putties and fillers that are created for use specifically with plastic kits. These are manufactured by the main plastic kit companies.

ABOVE: Two 'must have' items are a selection of plasticard and a cutting mat.

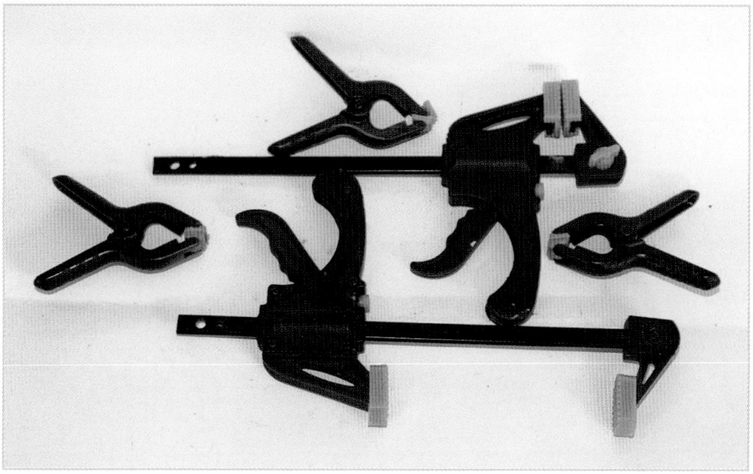

LEFT: Clamps are invaluable when joining two parts together that need to be held while the adhesive sets.

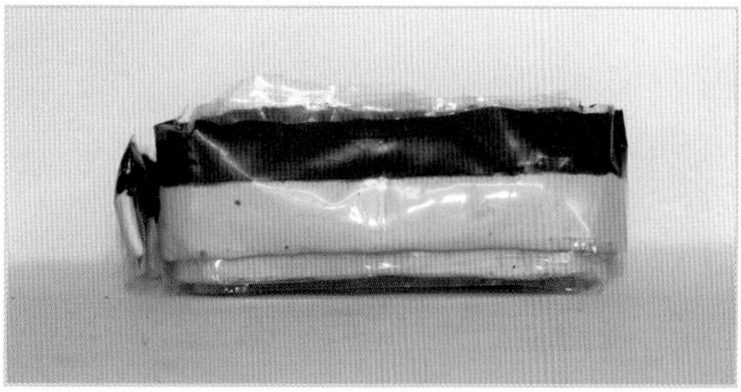

BELOW: Green Stuff is a two-part epoxy putty in yellow and blue that turns green when mixed together in equal amounts.

Glues

A wide variety of adhesives is available. PVA glue, widely available from both craft and DIY shops, is used in modelling and wargaming for scenic work on both figure and vehicle and weapon bases. Cyanoacrylate, otherwise known as 'superglue', is commonly used for bonding both resin and metal with ease. Care should be taken when using it as it will also bond skin and should be kept well away from the mouth and eyes. It is available from a host of outlets and as such is a readily available, very useful glue. The traditional and perhaps most widely used glue in modelling is polystyrene cement, which is made by several companies and is available in a variety of types, the most useful one being a liquid that is sold in a glass jar and comes with its own applicator, either a needle or brush.

A small selection of adhesives.

Paints

Paint is best stored in racks, which can be bought from any good hobby shop or online.

Acrylic paints can be used for painting figures, vehicles or aircraft. There is now much more choice of colours and brands than even ten years ago. Vallejo paints are highly recommended for their ease of use and colour range. These are well complemented by AK Interactive paints, which are available in a vast range of colours for figures, vehicles, aircraft and even naval vessels. They have introduced new paint sets that span several periods. Even a basic set will provide the main colours

ABOVE LEFT: A paint storage rack ensures that colours can be easily located when they are required.

ABOVE: Tamiya thinner for use with Tamiya paints: a bottle this size will go a very long way.

LEFT: A small selection of MIG pigments.

required and is a good starting point. These are the two brands of paint that feature most in this book, although alternative brands are available; Humbrol, for example, also make a good range of military-themed colours.

The advantage of acrylic paint is that it dries quickly, has little or no odour and the brushes and equipment used can be cleaned with water. The use of a good quality acrylic thinner is helpful for thinning paint so that it can be used in airbrushes. Tamiya acrylic thinner is recommended.

Weathering powders

Weathering powders are pigments in powder form that, when applied to a model, can create the effects of dust, rust, mud, soot and so on. They were initially manufactured by Mig Jimenez, whose superb AMMO range of weathering powders now gives the modeller a wealth of choice as to their desired finish. From replicating the effects of winter conditions or the harsh, arid desert of the Middle East, weathering powders help to achieve the appropriate finish.

Paintbrushes

Paintbrushes come in many shapes and types, from synthetic to high-end natural hair, from size 0000 (smallest) to size 6 (largest), and with a wide range of prices. Natural hair brushes in size 00, 0, 1, 2 are recommended: 00 and 0 for detailed work, size 1 and 2 for larger areas. Whatever type of brush you opt for these four sizes are ideal to start with. Just make sure that when you go to buy any brush you check that the bristles maintain a good point. If they fail to do so this could seriously impair your work and affect the overall finish. Even if you intend to airbrush your vehicles, you will still find a flat brush useful as this can be used for applying paint as well as achieving various effects such as dry brushing, which will be covered later.

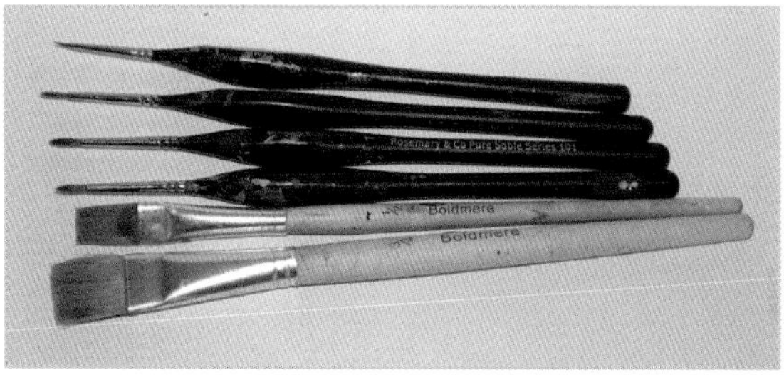

Airbrushes

There are many good makes of airbrush available, such as Aztek, Sotar, Badger and Iwata. Before you commit to one, do try out different brands as some may suit your painting style better than others. Buy the best model you can afford, along with a separate compressor. An inexpensive airbrush that uses

ABOVE: Pointed brushes are used for detailed work. Dry brushes are used for dry brushing and applying filters. Cleaning them well after use will extend their life.

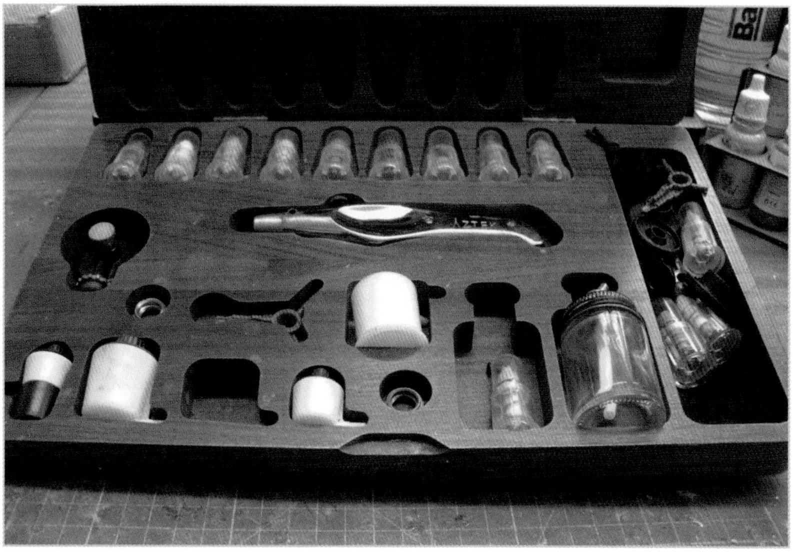

RIGHT: Using an airbrush will transform a painted finish.

Dried builders' sand for use during basing.

compressed air can look like a good option, but they are, in fact, a false economy as they provide an inconsistent pressure that has a negative impact on the final result. Once purchased take the time to master your airbrush, this tool will transform the finish of your models.

Basing

When used for either wargaming or for display, it is aesthetically pleasing to stage a figure or model on a well-executed scenic base. In addition to the equipment and materials already covered, there are a few things that are specifically needed for making bases or 'basing'. A sandy and/or rocky terrain can be created using dry builders' sand with dry cat litter to give extra texture. A realistic effect can then be achieved by painting this.

Once painted and highlighted, it is possible to add some grass, shrubs, flowers and small bushes. Static grass is good for achieving all-over coverage and comes in a variety of shades. It can be purchased from model shops and the internet. 'Tufts' of static grass can be used to create tall grass and small shrubs: these come in various sizes, heights and colours. Some even come with flowers of various colours, helping to add a little splash of colour to an otherwise drab scene.

Inexpensive paints, such as these, are ideal for creating paint effects on bases.

Small twigs taken from the garden and dried can also be used to add interest. The only limit is your imagination when it comes to scenic work. Small bricks can be very easily created for urban environments by cutting matchsticks to size and dying them with paint to the appropriate colour. If thin mahogany hardwood is used it is not even necessary to dye it.

This is a guide to the equipment required for modelling. If your budget is tight, start with just a few basic tools and a selection of brushes. You may not need everything listed above to begin with, but as your skills and confidence develop you will soon be using all the items and more.

A QUESTION OF SCALE

During the course of this book the reader will notice that there are frequent mentions of both figure size and scale. Wargames figures tend to be made to a certain height, such as 6mm tall, 20mm tall, 25mm tall and 28mm tall. Other sizes are available, but this book uses 20mm and 28mm tall figures. Larger figures (1:35 and 1:32 scale) are not really wargames figures, but are designed to complement vehicles of the same scale, so they are categorized by scale rather than height.

This is where some confusion creeps in. The main reason for categorizing wargames figures by height in millimetres and not by a set scale is that wargames figures are seen as playing pieces rather than scale models.

Categorizing wargames figures by height helps the customer to keep their collection consistent; 20mm figures, for example, will be roughly the same height even if purchased from a variety of different manufacturers.

Models, such as those produced by Airfix, are created to accurate scales so that multiple kits and figures can be incorporated together with all the elements at the appropriate size. At 1:72 scale (4.233mm to the foot), a figure of a modern man would stand 24.3 mm tall. This is a popular scale for aircraft modelling and is now widely used for the production of vehicle kits as well. 1:76 scale is a slightly smaller size (4.011mm to the foot) that is nearer to true 20mm wargames figures. This scale, also referred to as 'OO' scale, was first used for model railways and has subsequently been used to produce other models, such as the Milicast kits used in this book.

A comparison of figures commonly used in modelling and for wargames. From the left, in ascending order: 10mm tall, 15mm tall, 20mm tall and 28mm tall.

2 The Pacific, 1941–5

THIS CHAPTER COVERS THE modelling and painting of some of the units that the USA deployed to fight the war in the Pacific from 7 December 1941 to the Battle of Okinawa, which started on 1 April 1945. Over the years, the Pacific theatre has been a popular subject for Hollywood movies and is often portrayed as a United States Marine Corps (USMC)-only affair. In reality, there was a lot more to it than that, with the Army and Navy also involved. There were three main battles during this time: Wake Island, Tarawa and Okinawa. The US soldiers' uniform and equipment changed to meet the challenges encountered over this time.

Initially the uniforms worn by both the Army and the Marines looked very similar with both wearing the M1917A1 'Kelly' helmet, which was the M1917 Brodie helmet of WWI.

The A1 helmets had a modernized suspension system and production began in 1940; many WWI helmets were retrofitted to the new style. These were the helmets most likely to have been worn by the troops involved in action at Wake Island, Bataan and Pearl Harbor. The Brodie helmet was subsequently replaced by the well-known M1 helmet, which was used up to 1985.

US Marine Corps M1917A1 helmet.

The Springfield rifle model 1903 was the standard rifle issued to both Army and Marines. It was used by Marine units on Guadalcanal from August 1942 to February 1943 under Operation *Watchtower* (called by some marines 'Operation Shoestring', as they were issued with only enough ammunition for ten days when the operation began). The Springfield was replaced, first by the Army in the mid-1930s and later by the Marine Corps, by the M1 Garand rifle.

The uniforms changed as well. In 1941 they wore a khaki drill shirt and trousers with gaiters and brown boots for use in tropical climates. This then changed to the herringbone twill ('HBT') cotton uniform, which was a light serge green colour that faded to a lighter shade after repeated washing.

The Marine Corps adopted the M-1942 'Frog Skin' pattern camouflage uniform, also known as the 'Duck Hunter' pattern, which was first issued to Marine Raiders in 1942. After initial use, most Marines found the uniform uncomfortable and impractical to wear in the Pacific climate and preferred their 'HBT' uniforms instead. (It had been designed as a one-piece suit, without a back flap, which meant that answering a call of nature was a major undertaking and required taking off all the webbing.) Only the helmet cover continued to be widely used. The infantry units deployed in the Pacific wore a similar uniform to the Marines, but instead of the camouflage clothing they used a mix of USMC-type equipment, as well as Army issue.

For the most part this was an infantry war, but vehicles were used. The Landing Vehicle Tracked (LVT) was used in all amphibious operations and was adapted as time went on to meet the challenges that were faced during these landings. The M4A2 Sherman tank was deployed by the USMC in the Pacific: first at Tarawa in late November 1943, when Company C 1st Marine tank battalion (Medium) was landed on the island to support the landings there.

BATTLE-DAMAGED IWO JIMA M1 HELMET, SERGEANT ROBERT FILKOSKY

A US Marine Corps M1 helmet worn by Sgt Robert Filkosky, who fought in the Battle of Iwo Jima as a member of 3rd Battalion, 24th Marines, 4th MARDIV.

The WWII, US Marine Corps M1 helmet seen here was worn by Sgt Robert Filkosky during the Battle of Iwo Jima. He fought in the battle as a member of 3rd Battalion, 24th Marines, 4th MARDIV. During the fighting around the 2nd Airfield, on 23 February 1945, Sgt Filkosky was shot in the head and wounded. Two small calibre rounds penetrated through the front, right side of the helmet and exited the rear. The bullets furrowed the Marine's head, but did not mortally wound him. As he lay injured awaiting evacuation from the island, Sgt Filkosky witnessed the flag raising on Mt Suribachi. His helmet was recovered by a comrade and eventually placed in his overseas bag and returned to the United States. He has since kept the item as a unique conversation piece. During the 1950s the helmet was at one time displayed in Ripley's Believe it or Not Museum, St Augustine, Florida. Mr Filkosky later had the steel portion of the helmet bronzed for reunions, where he had fellow Iwo Jima veterans autograph the object in commemoration of their assault on the island. In an interesting adjunct to Mr Filkosky's history, he was a friend of his fellow 'I' Company member, the Academy Award-winning actor Lee Marvin.

The battle damage is remarkable, with two small entry holes from the rounds in the front of the helmet, amazingly close to one another. The helmet's camouflage cover is unique in that the 'I' Company, 3rd Battalion, 24th Marine Regiment tactical marking is clearly visible on the back of the helmet. There are no known helmets in the National Museum of the Marine Corps (NMMC) collection with WWII tactical markings. While the helmet's bronzing (hidden underneath the cover) is admittedly unusual, it is still an interesting feature of the helmet, as it contains the names of many Marine veterans who participated in the assault and have since passed away.

WAKE ISLAND, 8–23 DECEMBER 1941

Wake Island is a very important part of this story. It is a coral atoll situated 2,400km (1,500 miles) east of Guam, 3,200km (2,000 miles) west of Hawaii and 950km (600 miles) north of the Marshall Islands, which were held by the Japanese. Pan American Airways used Wake as a stopover for Clipper flights, which started in 1935, and so had a base there together with the US Navy. In January 1941 the island's defences were to be strengthened and civilian contract workers were brought in to do this. Unfortunately the work was not finished by the time of the Japanese attack, which started at noon on 8 December 1941.

The defenders consisted of some 450 officers and men of the 1st Marine Defense Battalion under Major James P.S. Devereux, 68 US Navy personnel and 1,221 civilian workers. Air cover was to be provided by twelve Grumman F4F-3 Wildcat fighters of Marine squadron VMF-211 under the command of Major Paul A. Putnam. In overall command was Commander Winfield S. Cunningham.

This is an important chapter of the story of the war in the Pacific, as it was at Wake Island that the Imperial Japanese Navy lost two surface vessels, the destroyers *Hayate* and *Kisaragi*. The *Hayate* was hit by a 3in shore-mounted naval gun, which penetrated the aft magazine with a shell, destroying the ship. After the garrison on the island had endured three days of Japanese air attacks, by 11 December the Japanese were sure that the defences had been sufficiently weakened to make it safe to start a landing.

However, that was not the case. The defenders held their fire until the Japanese were well within range of their 5in and 3in guns and then opened fire on the *Kisaragi*. The ship was sunk after a 100lb bomb hit the depth charge racks and the explosion blew off the stern. The bomber was a F4F Wildcat piloted by USMC Captain Henry T. Elrod. Wake Island finally fell after a second Japanese assault on 23 December, under circumstances that led to the press describing it as 'The Alamo of the Pacific'.

MEDAL OF HONOR, MAJOR HENRY ELROD, WAKE ISLAND

The Medal of Honor presented to Henry Talmage Elrod's widow for his heroic actions during the last days of the defence of Wake Island.

Henry Talmage Elrod was born on 27 September 1905, in Turner County, Georgia. After attending the University of Georgia and Yale University he enlisted into the Marine Corps in December 1927. He was appointed a Marine second lieutenant in February 1931.

Following more than a year at the Marine Corps Basic School in Philadelphia and at the Marine Barracks there as a student aviator, 2nd Lt Elrod was ordered to the Naval Station in Pensacola, Florida. There he served as a company officer and a student aviator. He was promoted to first lieutenant on 29 May 1934.

In February 1935 he earned his wings and, as a Marine Aviator, was transferred to Quantico, Virginia, where he served with a Marine aircraft unit until January 1938. In addition to his other duties, he was squadron school, personnel and welfare officer. He was promoted to captain on 1 September 1937. In July 1938 Capt Elrod went to San Diego for duty at the Naval Air Station and served as squadron material, parachute and personnel officer, until January 1941, when he was detached to the Hawaiian Islands area.

He arrived at Wake Island a short time before the hostilities commenced and was one of the twelve pilots who flew the Marine planes onto the island. During the defence of Wake, Capt Elrod repeatedly displayed conspicuous gallantry at the risk of his life, above and beyond the call of duty. On 12 December he single-handedly attacked a flight of twenty-two enemy planes and shot down two. On several flights he executed low altitude bombing and strafing runs on enemy ships, and became the first man to sink a major warship with small calibre bombs delivered from a fighter-type aircraft.

When his plane was destroyed by hostile fire he organized a unit of ground troops into a beach defence. Capt Elrod was killed in action defending Wake Island on 23 December 1941, repulsing repeated Japanese attacks until he fell mortally wounded.

Elrod was posthumously promoted to major in January 1942. On 8 November 1946 his widow was presented with the Medal of Honor, posthumously awarded to her husband for his heroic actions during the last bitter days of the defence of Wake. He was initially buried on Wake Island, but was reinterred in Arlington National Cemetery, Arlington, Virginia, in October 1947.

This chapter covers painting the Marines and Navy personnel who defended Wake as well the weapons they used, such as the .30 calibre medium machine gun and the .50 anti-aircraft machine gun. The figures and models used are all 1:72 scale metal and resin.

Modelling a Marine on Wake Island

Preparation

The first thing when painting any figure – metal, plastic or otherwise – is to take time to inspect it for mould lines and any flash left over from the moulding process. These can be removed using a small file and sharp knife. Then mount the figure onto either a temporary base, such as a piece of card or a bottle top, or straight onto its final base. Most wargamers use single bases for gaming WWII that are suitable for infantry figures. It is best to use temporary bases for weapons crews as this will help during the painting stages.

For this example, a 20mm figure is used, wearing the Brodie helmet, shirt, trousers, boots and light equipment as used on Wake Island.

Painting

Step 1. First the figure is painted with black, grey or white primer. In this case, a black primer was applied.

When the priming coat is fully dry, a thin, but even, coat of Vallejo 921 'English Uniform' is applied over the entire figure. This provides a good base colour for the uniform. Do not worry about painting over details such as the face at this stage, as these will be painted next.

A 20mm metal model of a WWII US Marine.

The figure has been primed and is ready to be painted.

The main base colour has been applied and the areas of flesh have been painted.

The uniform now stands out: leaving the darkest colours in the creases and areas such as around the seams of the pockets make the details show more clearly.

Highlighting is the addition of lighter tones of paint to the raised areas of the model, leaving darker tones in the areas that would naturally be in shadow.

The completed figure: all that needs to be done is to finish the base.

Step 2. The flesh areas are painted next. Start by selecting the flesh colour, in this case Vallejo 'Shadow Flesh', and use this as the base colour. Then take Vallejo 'Flat Flesh' and mix the two colours together in a ratio of 2:1. Use this to highlight the raised areas, nose, cheeks, lips, arms and hands, but take care to leave enough areas to act as shadow. Take more 'Flat Flesh', mixed in a ratio of 2:2 this time, and repeat the highlights. When properly dry, wash the flesh areas with sepia ink wash. When this is properly dry, highlight with undiluted 'Flat Flesh', taking care not to overdo this.

Step 3. Paint all the webbing and rifles next. Gunmetal is best achieved by first painting the metal parts of the rifle with black, then taking some Vallejo 865 'Oily Steel' mixed in a ratio of 2:1. Then highlight the raised areas. When fully dry, lightly paint the raised areas with undiluted 'Oily Steel' and finally wash with diluted black ink when dry. Paint in the wooden parts with a dark brown acrylic paint, and then highlight with Vallejo 'New Wood'. For the webbing, use AK3076 'Canvas Tone', from the AK Interactive set of US Army colours, and mix with Vallejo 819 'Iraqi Sand' at a ratio of 3:1. When dry, use a 2:1 mix for highlights.

Step 4. It is now time to paint the uniform. Start with AK3072 'Green Ochre', taking care to leave some of the base coat exposed in places that would naturally appear in shadow. Then mix some of the 'Green Ochre' with 'Iraqi Sand' at a ratio of 3:1 and use this for the first highlight. Repeat when dry, but this time use a mix with a ratio of 2:1.

Step 5. Once the uniform is painted, it is the turn of the smaller details such as helmet and rifle slings.

Vallejo 264 'Brown Violet' is recommended for use as the base when painting the helmets, highlighted with Vallejo 'Camouflage Green', mixed 2:1 and applied over dark green as a highlight. Paint the helmet bowl and rim, but leave a little area unpainted around the helmet where the bowl meets the rim.

Examples of 28mm Warlord Games USMC figures, painted using the same steps described in this chapter for the 20mm figures, have been included in the illustrations here for the very good reason that Okinawa was a joint Army and Marine operation.

USMC pilot

The garrison of Wake Island consisted of Marines, naval personnel who manned the coastal guns, and also pilots, who flew the USMC aircraft. Here are the steps to paint a 1:35 scale figure to depict one of those pilots.

Step 1. Start with a resin figure, which comes in kit form. These are simple to assemble using cyanoacrylate glue. Remember to clean away any mould lines before assembly.

Step 2. Paint the uniform using Vallejo 921 'English Uniform'. Next, paint the face and boots with Vallejo 818 'Red Leather'.

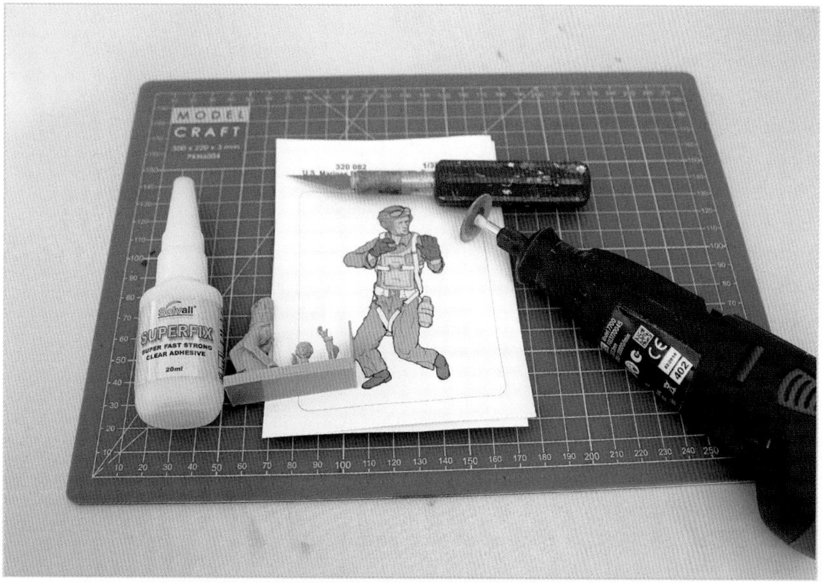

The USMC pilot kit.

Base coats have been applied to the face, boots and uniform.

These uniforms require less highlighting, but a little will improve the appearance.

Step 3. Cover the raised areas of the uniform using AK3082 'Dark Sand', taking care to leave some of the original base colour 'English Uniform' showing.

Next, paint the parachute harness with Vallejo 344 'German Winter Tank Crew White'. Using an ochre base coat, paint the pilot's lifejacket. These were actually yellow, so ochre is a good base colour.

Step 4. Paint the raised areas of the face, such as the forehead, cheekbones and nose, with Vallejo 860 'Medium Flesh Tone'. Take care to leave the base colour exposed in areas that would naturally be in shadow. For a realistic effect when adding the eyes, paint a small strip for each eye and then, using an off-white paint, add a small dot to the edge of each eye. Dark grey and off-white are used because black and white create a very stark effect that does not look realistic. When this is dry, finish the face by adding a tiny amount of white paint to the 'Medium Flesh Tone' and use this to highlight the forehead, cheekbones, chin and bridge of the nose.

Step 5. When the model is dry, paint the flying helmet: these were canvas and so were almost the same colour as the uniform. Paint the helmet with AK3082 'Dark Sand', taking care not to paint over the goggles, which should be left brown. Next add a small amount of white paint to this colour and use the mix to highlight the uniform. Add a little more white paint to this mix and use it to highlight the helmet.

Next, paint the parachute harness with white paint. The lifejacket is painted Vallejo 915 'Deep Yellow' and the belt is painted with Vallejo 988 'Khaki',

Details are added to the face.

highlighted with the same colour to which a little white has been added. Paint the gloves with 'Red Leather' and, when dry, highlight the gloves, boots and goggles with this colour, but with the addition of a small amount of white.

Step 6. Wash the boots, gloves and goggles with brown ink. When dry, paint the glass of the goggles, as well as any metal such as the belt buckle and parachute harness buckles, in Vallejo 720 'Gunmetal Grey'.

Modelling the heavy weapons

Both the Browning M1917 heavy machine gun and the Browning .50 calibre anti-aircraft machine gun were used by the troops defending Wake Island.

Step 1. Prepare the models by removing any mould lines and then construct them according to the instructions. Paint the guns using Vallejo 950 'Flat Black', as this will form a great base for a true gunmetal effect.

Details are added to the helmet.

HANDY TIP FOR PAINTING EQUIPMENT AND CREW

Even if the intention is to arrange your weapon and crew on a large base, it is best to base the models, even if only temporarily, on individual bases, such as bottle caps or paint tin lids. This will make the painting process much easier by allowing access to areas that could otherwise be difficult to see or reach.

The guns have been base-coated with black.

The weapons are now fully painted and matt coated.

Step 2. Once the base coat is dry, use Vallejo 264 'Brown Violet' and paint the weapons. Take care to leave black the areas that will be bare metal in the finished model. Also leave a little black exposed in the crevices of the machinery as this will give a more realistic effect. Next, create a mixture of 'Brown Violet' with Vallejo 'German Camouflage', using the ratio 1:2, and use this to highlight the areas already painted with 'Brown Violet'.

Step 3. Add Vallejo 865 'Oily Steel' to matt black paint at a ratio of 2:1 and use this to paint all the metal parts. Next, using undiluted 'Oily Steel', highlight the same areas and allow to dry. When properly dry, wash the metal parts with thinned black ink. Finally apply a matt varnish once dry.

Step 4. Paint any other details, such as ammunition belts. Two types of ammunition belt were supplied: disintegrating link and single belt. Disintegrating link belts were metal and mostly black in colour. The belt in this model is a disintegrating link and so the bullets should be painted first with gold paint, then a black band should be painted down the centre of the belt lengthways. Finally, that black strip should be highlighted with dark grey. Single belts are painted in the same way except they are khaki-coloured, not black.

USMC UNIFORMS AFTER WAKE ISLAND

By November 1943 Marines were equipped with the new HBT uniform. The M1942 'Frog Skin' pattern camouflage, first issued to Marine Raiders in 1942, was by now in widespread use by the USMC, though only really in use as helmet covers as the rest of the uniform was deemed inappropriate for the climate in the Pacific.

Tarawa was the first battle in the Pacific where LVTs were used to carry out an amphibious assault. The 2nd Marine Division had sufficient LVTs for the first three waves of troops at Tarawa, but then had to rely on the Higgins boat (LCVP) to land the following support waves. The LVT allowed troops to land directly on the beach as its tracks enabled it to lift out of the water. The Higgins boat, on the other hand, needed four feet of water in order to deliver troops onto a beach, which was to prove difficult at Tarawa.

The M4A2 Sherman tank saw action in the Pacific for the first time at Tarawa, with the tanks belonging to C Company 1st Corps Tank Battalion (Medium) proving themselves invaluable.

Tarawa, an atoll that is part of the Gilbert Island group, situated some 3,800km (2,400 miles) south-west of Pearl Harbor, was one of the bloodiest battles of WWII. The largest of its islets, Betio, is 4.8km (3 miles) long and 800m (0.5 mile) wide.

The attack on Tarawa was part of Operation *Galvanic*, an offensive that took place in the Central Pacific in order to secure a stepping stone to the Mariana Islands. Tarawa was an important target because it had an airfield and was of strategic importance to the outcome of US operations in the Central Pacific in 1943. It was defended by some 4,500 Japanese marines and troops from the 3rd Special Base Defence Force as well as the elite 7th Sasebo Special Naval Landing Force commanded by Rear Admiral Keiji Shibazaki. The island was extremely well defended with 100 pillboxes housing machine guns, as well as concrete positions housing guns of all sizes up to Vickers 8in. So confident was Rear Admiral Shibazaki of his preparations that he said 'it would take one million men one hundred years' to conquer Tarawa.

The 2nd Marine Division was assembled to attack the island, reinforced to some 18,000 men commanded by Major General Julian C. Smith as part of the V amphibious assault corps. Also part of this corps was the 27th Infantry Division, which was assigned to take Makin Atoll.

The assault on Tarawa began on 20 November at 05.05, when the US fleet opened fire on Betio (although commonly called the Battle of Tarawa, it was Betio that was attacked). The Marines got into their assault craft and waited until the three-hour barrage was completed. The landing craft then assembled for the run towards the beaches. Such was the intensity of the opening bombardment that the Marines wondered how anyone could survive such an ordeal, but the Japanese defences were well prepared. They soon started to return fire at the oncoming landing craft, resulting in many casualties. The first three waves landed on the beach with the aid of the LVTs. The following waves were in Higgins boats, but due to the tide they could not get over the coral reef and so the Marines had to wade some 500 yards to shore while under heavy fire. Once ashore, it was difficult to move inland, so heavy was the Japanese defensive fire that any movement from cover meant almost certain death. Some groups of Marines, showing extreme heroism, did manage to move inland assisted by the Sherman tanks, which had landed subsequently. The tanks took out Japanese-held positions with flame-throwers, grenades and satchel-charges. Even though they had established a foothold, the fighting continued until 23 November in the same savage manner as before. By the end of the battle the Japanese had lost some 4,690 soldiers with 17 captured, the Americans had lost more than 3,000 killed and wounded.

This brief account of the fighting on Tarawa indicates that without the LVTs and Sherman tanks the outcome would have been so much bleaker for the Americans.

US MARINE CORPS CAMOUFLAGE UTILITY COAT

This uniform coat was worn by US Marine Staff Sergeant Edward J. Driscoll Jr, who served with Company D (Scout), Second Light Tank Battalion during the Battle of Tarawa in 1942. This action marked the first widespread use of the new uniform by Marines in the Pacific War.

'Frog Skin' camouflage jacket worn by US Marine Staff Sergeant Edward J. Driscoll Jr.

Painting a US Marine

These examples use 20mm figures.

Step 1. As with all metal figures, first check for any mould lines and flash that can be left behind after the casting process. These can be easily removed with the aid of a small file and sharp craft knife.

Next, mount the figures on to bases for painting. Superglue is a good adhesive to use for this as it forms a good bond and only a small drop is needed. Then prime the figures with a suitable colour: grey or black are better primers for WWII uniforms as any subsequent colours applied appear darker than they would do if a white primer is used. A black primer will make subsequent colours look darker than a grey primer would.

Step 2. Once the priming coat has dried, block paint in the main uniform colours. Remember to leave a little of the darker primer showing to create shadows in appropriate places, for example where the arms are next to the body and between the face and collar of the jacket. In this example Vallejo 920 'German Uniform' was used. Next, the belt equipment and haversack are painted with AK3076 'Canvas Tone' from the set of AK paints designed for WWII US uniforms. The hands and face are then painted with Vallejo 'Red Leather'.

The face and hands are painted first, following the steps described above.

Step 3. The uniform to be seen in this model is of HBT type. Vallejo 'German Uniform' is a good base colour and should be applied to the entire uniform. Once dry, create a lighter tone of paint by mixing 'German

The two Marine figures have been blocked in and are ready for the next stage.

The flesh areas of the two figures are now complete.

PAINTING TIPS

To give a model both depth and definition, start by applying a dark primer. Take care not to paint over the dark primer in areas that would naturally be cast in shadow, such as under the chin, around the armpits and pockets. Then work from these areas to areas that would naturally catch the most light and paint them with the lightest shade. Keep the paint fluid and not too thick. It is better to use two thin coats rather than one thicker coat when painting figures.

Uniform' with some Vallejo matt white in a ratio of 3:1. Use this to highlight specific areas. Next, create a paler tone by mixing the paints equally and apply this to raised areas. Finally, mix the paints in a ratio of 2:3 and apply to only the most prominent areas. This should give your figure both depth and definition.

Step 4. Next move on to painting the weapons and webbing. Webbing colours did not change over this period so use the same process as outlined above for the Wake Island Marine. Be careful not to paint over the whole uniform when highlighting and leave enough of the darker base colour showing through to help create an illusion of depth. Use AK3076 'Canvas Tone' for painting the webbing and backpack.

The weapons are painted using the same methods described above for the Wake Island Marine's weapons.

Step 5. The next step is to create the camouflage effect. Most marines preferred not to wear the full camouflage suit, only the helmet cover, so this is what is covered here. These instructions, however, could be followed to paint the full camouflage suit.

First apply a base coat with Vallejo 'Luftwaffe Green'. Then highlight with a mixture of 'Luftwaffe Green' and Vallejo 'Green Grey' added 2:2. When dry, use Vallejo 924 'Russian Uniform' to paint small random blotches all over the area.

When these are dry, paint more blotches – taking care not to overpaint the previous work – of Vallejo 'Luftwaffe Green' with Vallejo 'German Camouflage Green' added at a ratio 2:1. When dry, repeat with blotches of Vallejo 'Light Brown'.

Next, apply some blotches of Vallejo 871 'Leather Brown'. When dry, wash over the area with sepia ink diluted with water at a ratio of 2:1 for a worn effect.

Rear view showing the backpack and other parts of the webbing equipment.

Front view of the same figures, showing the uniforms and webbing as well as the weapons, which have now been completed.

The completed figures and ground work on the bases.

The LVT1

This example is a 1:76 scale resin kit available from Milicast Models.

Tarawa was the first time these versatile vehicles had been used in a purely combat role. Before the assault on Betio (on Tarawa atoll) they were only used for logistics. They proved their worth at Tarawa as without them many more Marines would have been killed or wounded.

Step 1. Prepare the work area and equipment. The preparation of this model requires the use of a Dremel hand-held power tool with a fast and slow speed. This is invaluable for cleaning up resin models before painting. A facemask should also be worn when sanding or cutting resin. Carefully inspect the parts of the model and remove any excess flash with either a sharp craft knife or the Dremel. When finished, wash the kit in warm soapy water as this helps to remove any residue left over from the moulding process.

Carefully identify and lay out the parts.

Leave to dry at normal room temperature. Do not place on a radiator or use a hairdryer to speed up the drying process as excess heat can warp resin parts.

Step 2. Once the model has been cleaned and is ready to be assembled, place all the parts on a clear surface and refer to the instructions. This is also where a good reference source is invaluable.

Step 3. Once assembled, let the model dry for twenty-four hours, to ensure that the glue is properly cured. Next, inspect for any gaps or other defects that may require filling. The best filler to use for resin models is a two-part epoxy putty. Once the filler is dry, remove any excess filler/putty with very fine sandpaper.

Step 4. Prime the model using an appropriate primer and leave it to dry overnight. The AK Interactive paint set in US Army & USMC Camouflage colours (4220) provides a good range of colours for this model. The LVTs used at Tarawa were a blue/grey colour and AK4225 'Ocean Grey' is a very good match. Apply to the model using the airbrush. The best effect is achieved by spraying the paint on in several thin coats and, most importantly, allowing the paint to dry between coats to prevent runs in the paint. This part of the process will take some time to complete successfully and should not be rushed.

Step 5. The next step involves pin washing, which is a process that helps to reveal details more clearly. Dilute matt enamel dark brown paint with enamel

The constructed LVT before being primed.

This set of paints provides a good range of the colours required for vehicles.

Take care when applying paint. Use several thin coats rather than trying to use a single thicker coat of paint.

thinner at a ratio of 1:9. Then using a fine brush apply the wash to only the finer details of the model, for example allowing it to flow into joints and around wheels, taking care not to let any go onto any flat surface. Take your time to do this as pin washing well done can really enhance the finish of a model. Leave the wash to dry for at least twelve hours.

Step 6. Take the original base colour and add a little white paint at a ratio of 4:1. Then dip a large dry soft brush into this lightened paint. Wipe most of the paint off the brush using a paper towel or piece of card, so that only a hint of colour is left on the bristles. To test if you have the correct amount of paint left on the bristles, brush them across your hand and you should just see the raised areas lightly coloured. Once you are sure this is correct, proceed to brush the model lightly with the strokes all going in one direction only. This is called 'dry brushing' and gives the model a slightly faded look, while making the pin-washed areas stand out. Be careful not to overdo the dry brushing as too much will ruin the overall effect. Once completed, leave it to dry for a couple of hours.

Step 7. A filter is basically a translucent commercially produced ready-to-use colour that is applied to the whole model and has the effect of blending together all the previous work as well as adding a depth of colour that is essential to create a realistic finish. For a predominantly grey model, it would be best to use a blue filter. When using a ready-to-use filter ensure that it is mixed thoroughly before starting. It is also

A steady hand is required here, so take your time when working on a model during this stage.

Less is more when it comes to applying a filter: don't overfill the brush, using just enough to cover an area to achieve the desired effect.

Applying the filter to the model.

possible to dilute a small amount of the filter with enamel thinners to give more control over the final colour and so achieve the desired effect. Apply the filter sparingly using a large flat brush. The idea is to create a subtle effect, so do not flood the model with filter.

Step 8. Once the filter is dry, paint the tracks with a very dark brown acrylic paint, such as Vallejo 'Black Brown'. Take your time to do this and when complete allow the paint to dry thoroughly. Then apply a thin coat of gloss varnish for two reasons: this will help when applying decals, and a thin coat of gloss will help any subsequent washes to flow smoothly without pooling on the model.

Step 9. Next apply any decals required. In the case of this LVT, which is based on an actual vehicle, there was only a white star present on the sides of the vehicle. Applying water slide decals is straightforward if the instructions that come with them are followed. Once dry, a coat of matt varnish should be applied and left to dry, usually overnight. Varnish will help protect the paint during weathering.

Applying decals is covered in more detail in Chapter 6 in relation to applying decals to the M4A3E2 Jumbo.

Once dry, a second filter should now be applied, this time to any areas of shadow or where there are recesses. Use the same filter as before. When dry, paint in details such as tools, machine guns or lights.

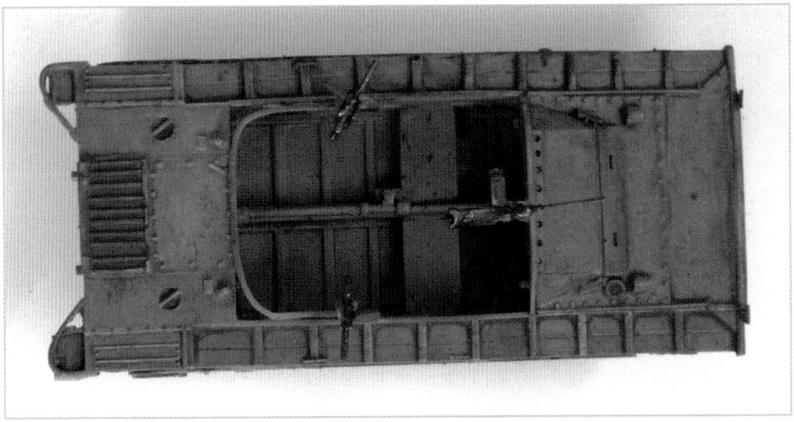

This view shows the troop compartment and the weathering that was added to achieve a worn effect.

LEFT: This side view shows the LVT with the stars applied. Note the weathering effect.

BELOW: Rear view of the completed model.

Step 10. Chipping is a technique that, while very useful, should really be kept to a minimum. If done too much the chips will be out of scale, yet if done to scale they would be too small to be seen. The model under consideration has not undergone chipping because these vehicles would have been fairly new at the time the battle took place, and so would not have shown much evidence of wear.

Step 11. These LVTs, however, would have shown some signs of wear from the troops they carried when walking on or inside the vehicle. Carefully go over these areas with a wash of dark brown enamel paint thinned down to the consistency of milk. Once this is done, apply a couple of coats of matt varnish with an airbrush. This will protect the work as well as eliminating any shine from the gloss varnish. For some models, it would now be appropriate to add a lighter dry brush or airbrush the whole model with a lighter colour. However, because the base colour of the example model is rather light to begin with, it is not really necessary to do any more than the pin wash, filter and weathering to achieve the effect desired.

The M4A2 Sherman tank

This M4A2 Sherman tank, the type used on Tarawa, is a 1:76 scale resin kit manufactured and sold by Milicast Models. It is going to be based on an actual vehicle: 'Colorado', a Sherman belonging to 'C' Company. The colour used in real life on these tanks was known as Olive Drab; Vallejo 264 'Brown Violet' provides a very good match.

Step 1. The first thing that needs to be done before construction and painting can start, and this goes for all resin kits, is to wash it first using mild detergent. Washing-up liquid is perfect when added to warm water. Then rinse and leave to dry.

Step 2. Once dry, check that all of the parts are present: with this kit there are only ten parts in total. Milicast make kits designed with the wargamer in mind, and wargamers like to get a model on the table quickly with the least amount of assembly required. Now start to put the kit together using cyanoacrylate glue with the assistance of some good reference sources.

Step 3. Next, prime the model. Grey primer is a good colour for priming models and gives a great key for paint. Leave the primer to dry for at least twenty-four hours.

Step 4. Then apply three thinned coats of Vallejo 'Brown Violet' paint with a brush. The paint will take a couple of hours to dry. Then pin wash the recessed details, for example around hatch covers, grilles and running gear.

Step 5. When the pin wash is dry, take some of the original colour, add a little white and dry brush the vehicle. This gives the finer details greater definition as well as creating a faded look. It also helps with the

ABOVE: The parts are laid out to check they are all present.

RIGHT: The model has been built: note the difference in colour between the turret and hull, which is normal with some resin kits.

The model with the base colour applied.

The pin wash should be done very sparingly, and should look subtle when completed. Any raised detail is then picked out with the dry brush for a worn paint effect.

next step, which is chipping. Using a sponge and some dark brown paint, dab the sponge lightly into the paint and then dab off most of the paint onto a piece of scrap paper, until only a trace is left. Go over areas of the model that will see wear, such as the areas where paint was likely to be damaged by hits from the likes of shrapnel and bullets, and the engine deck where the crew stood. Be careful not to overdo this, as less really is more and the intention is to achieve a subtle effect.

Step 6. Next apply a dark green filter, sparingly, over the entire model. Take care not to flood the model as only a light effect is required. A filter helps to create depth and bring out the base colour of the model.

Step 7. Once the filter is dry, paint in the details: use dark brown for the track and dark grey for the rubber on the wheels and tools. Lastly, any required markings are applied: in the case of this model, the name 'Colorado' together with a circus elephant, the insignia of the unit, were hand painted on. This is where pictures of the actual vehicle help, as not all the tanks of C Company were the same: some had names, others did not, but they all had the circus elephant, but painted in slightly different ways.

The green filter will adjust the colour of the paint.

A steady hand is needed here.

The effect of a light brush over the tracks with gunmetal will bring out the detail.

Step 8. Going over the track teeth with gunmetal paint helps to create the look of wear on these parts of the model. This can be a time-consuming task, so do not rush this.

Step 9. Now comes the fun part, weathering, although in this case it is a fairly simple task. Look at the model and really think about where the dirt, dust and mud would have collected. Using contemporary photographs and accounts will help with this. Tarawa was a very hot and dusty environment, only 130km from the Equator, with no mud. Pigment fixer is a clear liquid that fixes pigment to the model. Apply this to the running gear and tracks, in joins and joints, and any places where dust would collect. Be careful not to overdo it as you will ruin the effect. Take some MIG

LEFT: The pigment has been added to the model.

BELOW: The completed model.

BOTTOM: An M4A2 Sherman tank supporting Marines in 1944.

pigment powder and apply it with a large brush to the tracks and running gear first. This can be a messy job, so do it over a sheet of paper so that unused pigment can be collected for re-use. Then move on to the upper areas and repeat the procedure. The intention is to achieve the effect of gradation: the tracks and running gear are closer to the ground, so they would get more wear and more dust. The upper parts would, of course, be cleaner as they received less wear, but they would still be dusty.

Step 10. After the model has been allowed to dry for a couple of hours, take a large soft brush and go over the whole model to remove any loose pigment. The model is now finished.

OKINAWA, 1 APRIL – 22 JUNE 1945

The Battle of Okinawa lasted three months and saw some of the most bitter fighting of WWII: it was the largest concentration of Japanese artillery faced by American forces during the Pacific War. Operation *Iceberg* was the assault on the Ryukyu Islands, the largest of which was Okinawa, only some 550km (340 miles) from Japan. The taking of the island would give the Allies a base from which to launch the invasion of Japan itself.

To take Okinawa the Tenth Army was created: this was what is termed a 'cross army', consisting of the 7th, 27th, 77th and 96th infantry divisions of the US Army with both the 1st and 6th Marine divisions. The fighting on and around the island was very fierce and included mass kamikaze attacks on the Allied fleet. The Japanese fought desperately to stop the invasion of Okinawa as they knew if it fell it would bring the Allies just a stone's throw from their homeland. The fighting went on for eighty-two terrible days and resulted in 14,009 Allied deaths, the loss of 110,000 Japanese soldiers and a staggering 149,000 civilian deaths. The next operation would have been landings on the Japanese mainland, but this was not to happen as on 6 and 9 August 1945 Boeing B-29 Superfortresses of the 509th Composite Group, flying from Tinian in the Marshall Islands, dropped two atomic bombs, first on the city of Hiroshima and then on Nagasaki. WWII ended nine days later on 15 August following Japan's surrender to the Allies.

This is a hard plastic model of a soldier of the 7th Infantry Division in 1:32 scale using an Airfix multi-pose figure. The set consists of six figures in a variety of action poses, which gives the modeller a good variety of choice in choosing a subject.

The infantry was also used in many of the battles in the Pacific from 1941 to 1945. The basic uniform was similar to that used by the USMC, except that the infantry did not use camouflage. The uniforms worn by the figures in the Airfix set are pretty close to those of infantry units in 1945 in the Pacific.

Step 1. As these are plastic multi-part kit figures they will first need to be assembled.

Before assembly, clean off any sprues and mould lines using a sharp scalpel and a fine file. Assemble the figure using liquid polystyrene cement for the adhesive. Each figure comes with its own base, which is handy. The best way to assemble a figure is from the ground up in the following order: legs, then torso, arms, then head. Add the equipment next, starting with the belt, then the rucksack, followed by the helmet. No chinstrap or rifle sling is provided

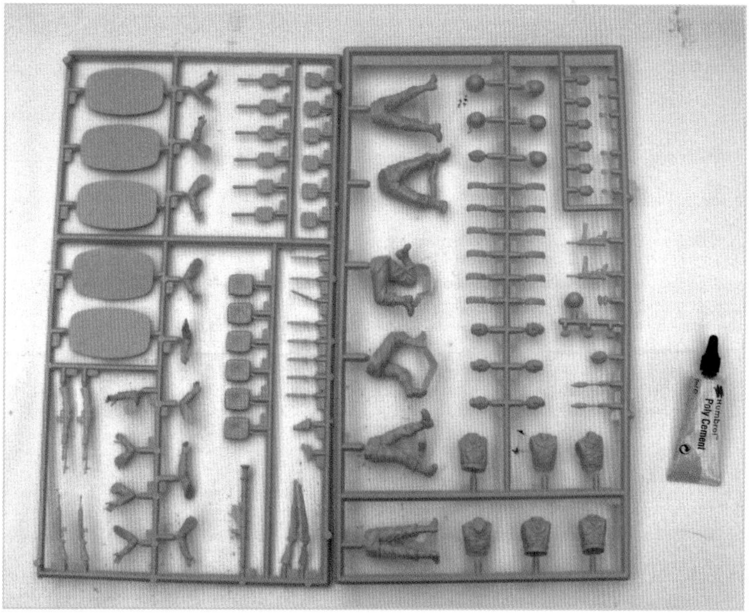

The sprue laid out: the glue to be used was supplied with the set.

with the kit, but these are easily built from scratch using paper cut to size and then glued in place with superglue. Next, with care, add the rifle, taking time to ensure that the figure holds the weapon in a realistic manner. Once completed, prime the figure.

Step 2. Before painting, be aware that, although this is a much larger scale figure than previous examples in this book, it will be more difficult to paint and achieve a realistic end result. On larger models, the colours need to be considered carefully: although the colours are the same as those used on the 20mm figure, they do need to be blended more to create a subtle effect.

Start by painting the face and hands with at least four shades of paint, going from dark to light to achieve the effect of depth. When dry, take some sepia ink, diluted with a little water, and wash this over these areas. This helps to create an extra layer of depth as well as blending the colours for a uniform look. When dry, add the eyes using a fine brush (such as 000) by painting two dark brown lines where the eye sockets are. Create the pupil by adding a white dot on either side of that line. Avoid using black as it is too harsh and makes the figure look as if it is staring.

Step 3. Once the flesh areas are completed, paint the uniform using Humbrol 155 'Olive Drab Matt' enamel. When this is dry, use 'Olive Drab Matt' mixed with a little Vallejo 819 'Iraqi Sand' in a 4:1 ratio to add highlights. HBT uniforms used by both the USMC and infantry had a blue hue, so to achieve the same colour add a very small amount of medium blue to the highlight colour. It just needs to be a hint of blue but no more than that. Once dry, lightly wash the uniform with diluted brown ink. Then highlight with the highlight mix again on the raised areas only.

Then paint in the belts and equipment as described above for the 20mm figures. Use the same colours, washed with diluted brown ink, which again creates depth. When dry, use the highlight mixture on the raised parts of the model's uniform only. When dry, finish the uniform by painting the buttons and helmet. Use Vallejo 264 'Brown Violet' for the helmet and add a little white to this colour to add highlights.

Step 4. Now paint the rifle, as described with the earlier figures, but wash the metal parts with a little black ink and the wooden parts with sepia ink for extra depth. Paint the insignia of the 7th Infantry Division on the left shoulder. The model is now almost finished. Give the figure several coats of good quality matt varnish, which seals the paint and protects the finished model. Once dry a base can be added to the figure.

FAR LEFT: The flesh areas have now been completed.

LEFT: The uniform has been painted.

The belts and equipment have been painted as well as the rest of the uniform.

The MDF base on which the finished figure is to be displayed is 40mm across.

The completed matt-coated figure is ready to be based.

3 North Africa and the *Torch* Landings

IN 1942 THE ALLIES were considering landings on mainland Europe, which was very much the preferred option for the Americans. The German forces in Europe, however, were strong and the Allies needed more time to prepare. After much discussion, it was finally agreed to go ahead with landings in North Africa. Known as the *Torch* landings, these took place on 8 November 1942 and involved more than 100,000 British and American soldiers. The American forces were under the overall command of Dwight D. Eisenhower, together with Major General George S. Patton Jr (whose units will feature in this book more than once) and Major General Lloyd Fredendall. The British forces were commanded by General Kenneth Anderson and Admiral Andrew Cunningham.

The landings and the following campaign saw many units deployed for the first time in combat, including Vichy French units, who went over to the Allied side after negotiations, Rangers and Paratroopers, as well as certain American tanks.

THE US INFANTRYMAN IN THE *TORCH* LANDINGS

The US Infantry that landed on the African coast during Operation *Torch* were unsure how the Vichy French forces they were to meet would react to them. They hoped the Vichy French would come over to the Allied side without conflict, but this was not the case and Vichy French forces put up resistance that lasted several days.

The uniform that was issued to Infantry units was largely the same as the HBT issued to the Army and Marines in the Pacific. The US Army thought that as the campaign was in Africa, the weather and climate would be warmer than indeed it really was (the same assumptions have been made in more recent times with other nations). In fact, the campaign took place during the winter and the weather was changeable and wet, with freezing nights. This left the troops gathering together sweaters and any warmer items of clothing they could find in an effort to keep warm.

An M3 Lee crew takes a moment to resupply in an olive grove, Tunisia, 1943.

A particular feature of this uniform was the wearing of a brassard – or armband – on the left arm. Displaying the stars and stripes, its purpose was to enable the easy identification of American troops from other Allied troops, and was used in other campaigns when American troops were to operate with Allied nations.

During the following campaign in North Africa the HBT uniform was steadily replaced by the M41 Spencer jacket, M37 wool trousers and the M37 woollen shirt, the uniform that is most closely associated with the GIs of WWII. No doubt this was warmly welcomed by those cold GIs who still wore HBT during the *Torch* landings.

The figures with the new paper brassard.

A grey primer has been applied.

Modelling the US Infantryman in the *Torch* landings

These five 1:56 scale US infantry models will be painted wearing HBT and staged as if they were participating in the *Torch* landings in November 1942. They are highly detailed, hard plastic multi-part figures manufactured by Warlord Games in the UK. They require little preparation, other than a wash in mild soapy water, then on to construction.

Step 1. Build each figure from the bottom upwards: attach the lower torso and legs to the supplied base, then the upper torso, then head, and then attach the belt equipment. This example will construct four riflemen, an NCO with a rifle (up to 1944, the M1 Garand rifle was the main weapon issued to all ranks below lieutenant; the Thompson submachine gun was not as common at that time) and a fifth figure with a Browning Automatic Rifle (BAR). This helps to identify the relevant part for each figure.

Step 2. The next step is to deal with the models' arms, as these are not attached until the brassard is added. Make the brassard from a thin strip of paper, then attach it to the left arm with diluted PVA glue and allow to dry. Once the brassard is dry, fit the arms ensuring that they are matched with the correct weapon so a realistic 'action' pose is achieved. Once you are satisfied with the placement of the arms and weapons, glue them in place and leave to dry for a few hours.

Step 3. Prime the figures with grey primer. When dry, add a little white to Vallejo 920 'German Uniform' and brush this all over the figures with a broad brush.

When thoroughly dry, wash the figures with dark green ink as this adds depth to the uniform and helps achieve an effective overall end result. When the wash is dry, highlight with Vallejo 'German Uniform' to which a little white paint has been added. Allow plenty of time to do this carefully, in order to achieve a sense of depth and some much-needed definition to the uniform.

When the uniform has been painted, the webbing, belt equipment and backpack should then be painted with AK3072 'Green Ochre'.

Add some Vallejo 847 'Dark Sand' to the 'Green Ochre' and use this to highlight the webbing, belt equipment and backpack. Add some more 'Dark Sand' to this mix and repeat the process, this time highlighting only the areas that are most prominent.

Step 4. Now proceed to paint the face and hands with Vallejo 818 'Red Leather' as the basecoat. When this is dry, mix 'Red Leather' with Vallejo 955 'Flat Flesh' in a ratio of 50:50 and use this to paint the raised areas of the face and hands, leaving some of the base colour exposed in creases, around the nose and between the figures. Add a little more 'Flat Flesh' to this mix and then highlight the previous work again. When dry, use a flesh-coloured ink wash over the areas of the face and hands, which will blend all the previous colours together for a natural look. When dry, highlight the raised areas of the face and hands for a final time.

ABOVE LEFT: Base coats have been applied.

ABOVE RIGHT: The wash helps bring the uniform highlights together.

LEFT: Wooden handles are painted together with any areas of gunmetal.

The brassard has been painted.

Step 5. Add a base coat of Vallejo 846 'Mahogany Brown' to all the wooden parts on the figure, such as the rifle, spade and bayonet handle. Paint any metal work with Vallejo 898 'Dark Sea Blue'. Highlight the wooden parts with Vallejo 311 'New Wood', then add a little 'Flat Flesh' to this to further highlight these areas on the rifle, spade handle and bayonet grip.

Pick out the buttons with 'Dark Grey' and highlight with 'Gunmetal'. Paint the chinstraps on the front of the helmet with 'Khaki', and those on the rear with 'Strap Red Brown'. (The M1 helmet had a liner that fitted into the outer shell, which explains the presence of the two tapes, with one at the front and the other at the rear.) Paint any camouflage netting with 'Khaki'.

Finally paint the brassard: first with a base coat of 'Light Grey', then a coat of white. Next paint the blue field 'Dark Blue', then the red stripes and finally the white stars.

This will provide an authentic looking figure of a GI as seen during the *Torch* landings in November 1942.

The finished models.

M3 Half-Track

The early version of the M3 was manufactured by three companies: White Motor Company, Diamond T and Autocar. Some 15,000 standard M3s and more than 38,000 variants were produced during WWII. The troops who used the first M3s dubbed them 'Purple Heart' boxes. This nickname was derived from the lack of overhead protection as well as the thin armour, meaning that the occupants were at risk of receiving injuries even while inside (the Purple Heart is the medal awarded to recipients wounded in combat). General Omar Bradley investigated these claims and stated in his report that too much was being asked of the new half-track by troops who were unfamiliar with it. The M3 and the later model M3A1 continued in service and saw widespread use during the rest of the war. The difference between the M3 and M3A1 was the addition of a pulpit on the right-hand side of the driver position for the AA machine gun, while the M3 had just a pedestal mount. Through 1942–3 all M3s were slowly upgraded to the M3A1 specification.

Modelling the M3 half-track

This vehicle was used throughout the North African campaign but especially during Operation *Torch* in 1942 when the American-crewed tanks were the first in the war to engage in tank versus tank combat against the Vichy French R35s. It is a 1:72 scale Italeri kit that can be enhanced by the addition of a superb aftermarket accessory set made by S&S Models.

Step 1. Construct the kit as per the instructions, but leave the upper and lower halves of the kit separate until the glue is properly set and then join them together. Next, select the items required from the accessory set, such as the side stowage racks, rear stowage racks, a few boxes and rolled up tarps, and clean them with a fine file before attaching them to the M3 with cyanoacrylate glue.

Step 2. After priming the model with grey primer and allowing this to dry, apply a base coat of Vallejo 887 'Brown Violet' with a brush.

TOP: The model now with metal stowage added.

ABOVE: Start to construct the kit but leave the upper and lower halves of the vehicle separate until the glue is properly set.

RIGHT: The model has been given an even coat of olive drab.

Highlights are applied with a lighter tone of paint. Do not overdo this stage, as too much will ruin the finish.

The wash has both toned down the original colour and helped to bring out the detail.

When dry add some white to the base coat and brush this lightly over the raised areas and panels. When dry, apply a wash of dark brown.

When the wash is dry, dry brush the vehicle again lightly with a mixture of 'Brown Violet' and a little white paint. Go over the whole vehicle paying particular attention to the areas that will catch the light. Be careful not to overdo this as a subtle effect is desired.

Step 3. Now paint the stowage and tools in appropriate subdued colours. Bright colours will be difficult to blend in later and will stand out too much. Highlight the stowage with the colours used before, but now mixed with a little Vallejo 'Iraqi Sand'. Paint the .50 calibre heavy machine gun with gunmetal, and when dry, wash with two coats of black ink.

Wash over the wooden boxes, tool handles and other stowage with dark brown ink diluted 50:50 with water. This will darken these items.

Now paint the wheels and tracks with Vallejo 306 'Dark Rubber'. This is a good colour to use because the tracks on the M3 were made from two cables sandwiched between two lengths of rubber, then pressed together at high temperature, thus forming the tracks. They were non-metal tracks and so should be painted like rubber.

Step 4. When the model is dry apply a coat of satin varnish. When this is dry any decals can be applied. This is best done over a shiny surface, which is why satin varnish is ideal. For tips on the application of decals see the model of 'Cobra King' in Chapter 6. In this example some decals have been added from the Mirage Hobbies kit of the M3 Lee medium tank (*see* below).

The decals will be dry after around four to five hours in a warm room. Apply an even coat of matt varnish to the entire model. The varnish will both protect the decals and provide the perfect surface for weathering the model. MIG Pigments P038 'Africa Earth' is used for the lower areas, such as the tracks, running gear and wheels, and MIG P037 'Gulf War Sand' is used on the upper areas. Once the weathering has been completed, add any passengers.

ABOVE: Paint the stowage boxes in muted colours, such as olive green and shades of olive drab and brown.

RIGHT: Gunmetal was rather dark. A machine gun should not look too bright, but have just a hint of steel showing here and there.

Here the tracks have been painted dark grey.

The completed M3 with a 20mm crew added from AB Figures.

T12 GMC Tank Destroyer

The campaign in North Africa saw the first use in combat of a new vehicle, the tank destroyer. Several types were produced as the war went on, but the first one was the T12 GMC or, as it was also known, the M3 75mm Gun Motor Carriage. This vehicle came about from the need to have an armoured tank destroyer. It followed the M6, which was a Dodge weapons carrier mounted with a 37mm anti-tank gun, but this design was unpopular as it was both under-gunned and lacked armour. The solution was to mount an M1897A4 75mm gun, which was the American version of the famous quick-firing French '75', on an M3 half-track fitted with a shield. Eighty-six vehicles were produced in August and September 1941.

The T2 was first used in combat in the Philippines in early 1942 to provide fire support at Bataan, where there were few Japanese tanks deployed. Their first significant use was with the 601st Tank Destroyer Battalion, a mixed unit of T12s and M6s, during Operation *Torch* and the subsequent campaign in North Africa in 1942. In March 1943 the 601st TD Battalion went into action at El Guettar, where it held off a German attack by some 100 tanks and claimed to have knocked out about thirty, including two of the then new Tiger 1s, for the loss of roughly twenty T2s. This one engagement proved the worth of the T2 and helped start a line of American Tank Destroyers that arguably helped delay the advent of the heavy tank until late 1944. When correctly used the American tank destroyer was a formidable opponent.

Modelling the T12 GMC Tank Destroyer

From a wargaming perspective the modelling possibilities are varied as there are examples of the T12 in most ranges from resin to metal. The example used here is made by Italeri and comes in a box of two 'Quick build' kits that are easy to assemble. Adding a few tweaks here and there can bring the basic model up a notch or two.

Step 1. Start by having a good look at the kit and read through the instructions.

Still attached to the body parts is the plastic sprue left over from the injection moulding process. This should be removed using a pair of strong cutters.

As the kit is to be glued, the two locating pins on the reverse side of the floor unit can be removed. Using a fine drill bit and pin vice, drill out a small portion of the barrel as this will give a much more realistic look.

Step 2. Assemble the rest of the kit following the instructions provided. It is easy to make the model more realistic by creating and adding some stowage, especially as, when in use, these vehicles were festooned with all sorts of items from bags to rolled-up tents.

The two lockers that were commonly located by the rear door on T12s are not included with this kit, but they can be easily scratch built using plastic card.

Starting with 30 thou plastic card, the outlines are scratched out directly using a blade. Two pieces 8 × 7mm are required, so mark these and then cut them.

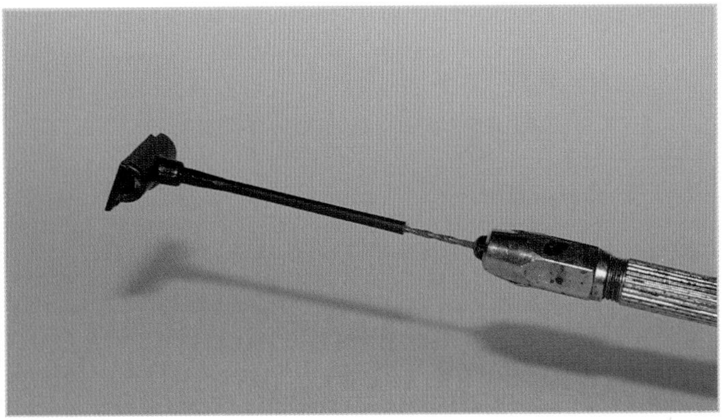

ABOVE: Remove the plastic left over from the injection moulding process.

LEFT: Drill a small portion of the barrel out to give a more realistic look. (This is a barrel from the M36 Jackson, but the process is the same.)

The pieces now cut to size.

Side pieces, 3mm wide, are then required for the four sides of each locker, so eight pieces are needed altogether. Cut them to length to match each side, less 1mm for the top and bottom pieces (these should be 6mm long).

The pieces are then assembled. Each locker had three hinges and a lock. To make these, lightly scribe down the long side of each locker 1mm from the outer side. Then add the hinges from small pieces of plastic card along the scribed line. The lock is also a small piece of plastic card and should be positioned at the same height as the middle hinge, but on the opposite side of the locker.

Step 3. To paint the model, follow the steps for the M3 halftrack.

The assembled lockers.

The T12 complete with the new lockers and stowage. This is a simple addition that adds an extra level of much needed detail to a good, but plain model.

BELOW: The finished model T12.

M3 Lee Medium Tank

The M3 Lee medium tank became operational in late 1941. It was intended as a design that could be built as quickly as possible and was armed with a 75mm gun. It was also produced with a British pattern turret, in which form it was known as the Grant. The M3 was deployed in North Africa, including in Tunisia.

Modelling the M3 Lee Medium Tank

This 1:72 scale model is made by Mirage Hobbies. It comes with several options of main gun. For this example, which replicates a vehicle that fought at the Kasserine Pass in February 1943, a gun stabilizer will be added by placing a weight at the end of the 75mm gun.

Step 1. Before building the kit, take a good look at the plans and become familiar with the various steps of its construction.

Start with the lower hull and running gear, which are always assembled first. Leave the glue to cure overnight before moving on to the rest of the build. This is important as the superstructure is next and this will need a firm base on which to build.

Now start on the upper hull, taking care to dry fit the parts first before trying to glue them into place. This way any fine adjustments can be made without difficulty. Use a good quality sharp blade at all times as well as a pair of cutters.

Once completed, leave the upper hull to dry before moving on to the turret.

RIGHT: The M3 Lee kit.

BELOW: Start to assemble the model. At this point you need to decide between an open or closed turret.

The assembled model. It is easier to add the tracks after the running gear and road wheels have been painted.

LEFT: The primed model is now ready to have the stowage added.

BELOW: An even coat of olive drab is applied.

Step 2. Before starting, it is necessary to decide if the finished model is to have an open or closed turret. This example will have an open turret so the crew can be placed inside. Take time to assemble the turret, as the parts are delicate and can easily be broken.

It may be that the exhaust mufflers are a better fit if the plating that covers them is assembled first.

Do not fit the tracks at this time, however, because leaving them until later will make it easier to paint the running gear and road wheels. The tracks can now be primed with grey primer.

Leave the model to dry out for a day to ensure that the glue is fully cured. Apply filler to any gaps and allow this to dry fully before sanding.

RIGHT: A dark brown wash is now applied.

BELOW: The stowage items are now painted.

Step 2. Next add some stowage to make the model look 'lived in'. Once done, prime the model with grey primer. Leave to dry overnight and then apply an even coat of MIG 926 'Olive Drab' dark base.

To continue painting this model, follow the steps as described for the M18 (*see* Chapter 6). For advice on weathering, please follow the steps for the M4A2 Sherman (*see* Chapter 2). The pigment colours required for weathering are MIG P038 'Africa Earth' for the lower areas and P030 'Beach Sand' for the upper areas.

The completed M3 Lee. No American tank of the Operation *Torch* campaign would be complete without the yellow band, which is supplied as a decal with this kit.

The completed M3 Lee, now with its crew and base, taking a chance to refuel in an olive grove in Tunisia.

M3A1 Stuart Light Tank

The M3A1 Light Tank was produced from May 1941 and was a much-improved model over the earlier M3. This had a riveted turret, which proved dangerous when the turret was hit as the rivets would 'pop' off with some force and injure the crew. The second difference was the addition of a gun stabilizer for the 37mm gun.

The M3A1 was also called the Stuart, named after the American Civil War General J.E.B. Stuart; its unofficial name was 'Honey', which was coined after a test driver called the light tank 'a honey to drive'. The 1st and 2nd Armoured Divisions, both equipped with Stuarts, landed during the invasion of North Africa: the 1st Armoured Division had two battalions with both M3 and M3A1 Stuarts, while the 2nd Armoured Division had the new M5 Stuart.

The 1st Armoured Division landed at Oran on 8 November 1942. The next day the first armoured clash of the campaign began when they met a force of Vichy French R35 tanks outside Oran. During the fighting the French lost fourteen tanks, but the Americans came off lightly with damage to only one M3A1.

It was not until the Americans came up against German tanks that they quickly realized that M3A1 and M5 were no match for the Panzer Mk3 or the Mk4. Subsequently the lighter Stuarts were used as flank guards for the M4 Sherman battalions and for reconnaissance work, for which the fast and manoeuvrable tank was well suited.

Modelling the M3A1 Stuart Light Tank

This is a kit from The Plastic Soldier Company, whose products are purely designed with the wargamer in mind and as a result create a very robust model. Included in the kit are the parts for three variants of the M3 used in the Pacific (M3 early production), Tunisia or Italy (M3A1 mid-production), and by the British in North Africa, where the 8th Army used a very large number of the M3 'Honey' (M3A1 late production). As the instructions provided need to cover the construction of the three variants, they can at times seem confusing. Read them through carefully before starting with the help of photos of the chosen variant. This will help identify the parts needed as well as such details as whether the model requires additional fuel tanks.

Step 1. Select the parts for the Tunisian version, the M3A1 mid-production, and follow the instructions given in the kit for the construction as they are very straightforward. Do be aware that the turret, once constructed, may be too large to fit into the hole provided in the hull. Using a very sharp craft knife, enlarge the hole very slightly so that it can accept the turret.

A modification worth considering for this model is the replacement of the kit-supplied 37mm gun barrel, which seems to be out of proportion, with a turned brass one from the Polish company RB Model, which has an English-language website. These replacement gun barrels are highly crafted and very reasonably priced, but they make a real difference.

Step 2. The only part of painting the M3A1 that differs from the previous vehicles covered in this chapter is the yellow band around the turret. This also features on the Lee and was a common feature of markings on early American tanks up to mid-1943.

Step 3. Finish the model in the same way as the other vehicles in this chapter. Remember, when using any weathering product, less is more.

LEFT: Use a sharp blade and remove a small amount of plastic evenly from the inside of the turret ring.

The aerial was fitted here using fine wire.

A PAINTING BASE

When working on artillery pieces or on a gun, after they are built and primed it is a good idea to mount it on a base for painting. This makes it easier to handle and helps prevent any damage to the model. It is good practice to always base any models together with their crews. Weathering should be done after the base has been painted and scenery added. This will help the model blend into the base, as in real life the gun should be part of the scene and not look separate.

The M3A1 Stuart with a new brass barrel as well as an antenna.

M2A1 105mm Howitzer

The M2A1 Howitzer must be one of the most well-known medium artillery pieces of WWII and an updated version is still in service in the US Army. The M2A1 has been used by many countries postwar.

The M2A1 started life as the M1 in the early 1920s. This became obsolete in 1935 and the M2 was developed by changing the chamber dimensions. It was standardized in 1940 after being redimensioned and having a new trigger shaft added: this was now the M2A1. It was a very useful and versatile gun and became the standard artillery piece used by the US Army in all theatres of the war. It was issued to both infantry and armoured divisions, for whom it was mounted on the chassis of an M4A3 Sherman and named the M7 or 'Priest'. The range of the M2 was some 11,000m (12,205 yards). It could fire both 33HE shells and a 29.29lb HE-AT shell. The muzzle velocity was 1,450m/s (1,550 yards/s) and penetration was 115mm at all ranges.

Modelling the M2A1 Howitzer

The M2A1 is the gun that was issued to all infantry divisions from 1940 onwards. This is an all-metal kit available from S&S Models and no assembly instructions are included. Although it may look like a simple kit at first glance, there are several parts that need to be assembled in a certain way.

Step 1: As this is an all-metal kit, some patience is required when assembling it. Unlike a standard plastic kit, cyanoacrylate glue is required and this will take time to cure, typically about an hour to fully achieve a good strong bond. With this in mind, assemble the kit starting with the wheels and then gun trails.

Now fit the barrel and make sure it is a good fit. Once this is achieved, glue it into position and ensure that the parts are fully supported while the glue cures.

Step 2. Now assemble the gun shield. This is a two-part shield, unlike others used on pieces of this type. Glue the pieces together and support them while the glue cures. Consult good reference sources throughout the build as this will help you locate and attach the parts in the correct place.

Attach the shield to the gun using the glue and again ensure it is fully supported while the glue

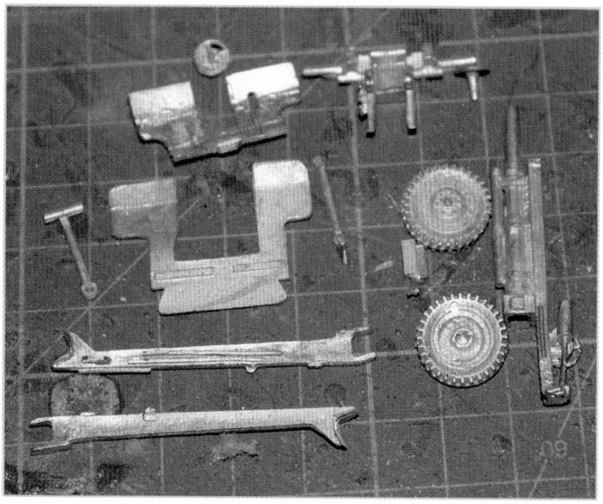

The parts required to build the N2A1 Howitzer.

The trails have been fitted.

Support the barrel while it dries. The other parts are ready to add.

LEFT: The constructed model gun.

BELOW: The M2A1 is now ready to paint.

cures. Then fit the tow bar and hand spike to the end of each trail. Good reference sources, such as the internet and books, should be consulted to confirm that the pieces are correctly placed: the tow bar goes on the right and the hand spike on the left side when the model is viewed from the rear. The M2A1 is now ready for painting.

Step 3. The standard colour for all US Army vehicles and guns was, of course, olive drab, so use Vallejo 889 'Olive Brown', which is a very good match. Follow exactly the same process as for painting a vehicle. Paint the model first, then the tyres and follow by weathering and so on.

Step 4. Once the gun has been weathered, add the crew and then start the ground work of the base. When the ground work has dried and been painted, add a little grass and scrub (this topic will be covered in more detail in Chapter 8).

LEFT: It is important to take time when painting tyres. Never use black as it is too harsh; dark grey is a much better choice.

BELOW: The completed gun with a 20mm crew from AB Figures.

Sicily and Italy, 1943–5 4

THIS CHAPTER COVERS THE American forces engaged in the campaigns in Sicily and Italy, which ended on 2 May 1945. The units that saw action in both Sicily (9 July–17 August 1943) and the subsequent campaign in Italy (3 September 1943–2 May 1945) will feature here. Infantrymen, of course, were deployed in both campaigns, but the nature of the terrain made the use of specialist units invaluable: these were the Rangers and Airborne forces in Sicily and later the Rangers in Italy.

Operation *Husky*, the invasion of Sicily, saw the widespread deployment of Allied paratroop units, as well as Ranger units. The Ranger units attached to the 7th Army under General George S. Patton were the 1st, 3rd and 4th Ranger Battalions. This operation was the first time such a large number of Ranger units had been deployed.

The 82nd Airborne Division, under the command of Major General Matthew Ridgway, was known as the 'All American' from a belief that the Division had men from every state in America. The initial assault, made by the 505th Parachute Regimental Combat Team under Colonel Gavin, was the first regimental-sized combat parachute assault conducted by the US Army in WWII. The 82nd proved itself to be a true elite unit during the landings. In November 1943 it was sent to the UK to prepare for the invasion of Europe.

The three Ranger Battalions deployed in Sicily were trained by Colonel William Orlando Darby. He was one of the first American troops to be sent to Northern Ireland, where he became acquainted with the training methods of the British Commandos. A US Army equivalent was sanctioned on 19 June 1942 and the 1st Battalion was recruited for training in Carrickfergus. Most of the recruits came from the 34th 'Red Bull' division. Darby later commanded the 1st Battalion in Italy. This became known as Darby's Rangers (although the Italians in Sicily nicknamed it the 'Black Death'). Darby's Rangers fought throughout the Italian campaign: Darby himself was killed two days before the Germans surrendered.

M15 ANTI-AIRCRAFT HALF-TRACK

The M15 T28E1 was an anti-aircraft version of the M5 Half-track. Eighty were produced for use in the North African campaign and some of these were also used in Sicily and Italy. The M15 could provide both anti-aircraft fire and ground support from its 20mm cannon and two .50 calibre M2 heavy machine guns, because the guns were mounted in a traversable turret in the back of an adapted M3 Half-track.

Modelling the M15 Anti-Aircraft Half-Track

This is a metal kit made by SHQ Miniatures. Because it is not a true modellers' kit, care is needed when assembling it as the plan assumes pre-existing skills and knowledge. Good reference material is essential.

Step 1. As with the Lee (*see* Chapter 3), the kit is assembled starting with the running gear, and then the cab and seats. Leave the glue to cure for a couple of hours. Unlike polystyrene cement, cyanoacrylate glue cures properly in only a couple of hours and so is faster to work with, but care needs to be taken in order to avoid any accidents.

Step 2. Now assemble the gun cradle and then add the guns. Do this in two stages and take care with all the parts as they are small and delicate. Now leave the gun cradle and progress with the rest of the build: the reason will soon become apparent. Once the two halves of the model have been joined, with the cab attached to the rear section, and allowed to dry, add the fenders, the lights and armoured visor. The support legs for the visor were not properly formed and this was corrected using brass rod, cut to length. Locating holes were drilled with a pin vice to correspond with the positions of the new support legs: these should ensure a strong and stable bond.

RIGHT: The M15 Half-Track under construction.

BELOW: The parts for the anti-aircraft gun and its housing.

The assembled gun mounted on the back of the half-track.

Step 3. Now move on to the turret. The instructions show ammunition stowage boxes, but as these were not included in the kit they were scratch built. Cut four pieces of plastic square rod each 5mm in length and then cut these in half, giving eight pieces in total. Glue four on the inside of the turret, either side of the guns. These were dry fitted first so the correct location of the new boxes could be judged correctly.

Step 4. The kit comes with the option of a roller for the early M15 or a winch for the later M15. This model will be fitted with the roller as these were more common in both Sicily and Italy. Next, fit the headlights by drilling a small hole in the locations marked. Add the stowage next and then prime the model: as this is an all-metal kit the use of car primer is recommended and this can be bought from any good car accessory outlet.

ABOVE: The armoured visor.

LEFT: The primed vehicle, ready for painting.

BELOW: Apply two thin coats of acrylic Olive Brown.

Step 5. Now give the model two thin coats of acrylic Vallejo 889 'Olive Brown'. Once dry, add a little white to this colour and use it to add highlights to the panels. This will give the effect of shade and depth to the model.

Step 6. Apply a green acrylic filter (Vallejo) over the model: take care to do this sparingly and evenly with a brush. This product should dry fairly quickly and gives a pleasing result. Once dry apply a coat of satin varnish with an airbrush.

After a green acrylic filter has been applied and allowed to dry, use an airbrush to apply a coat of satin varnish.

Apply a very light coat of brown filter with a brush dipped in enamel thinner.

Step 7. Apply brown filter sparingly with a brush lightly dipped in enamel thinner. The brush should only be moist, so wipe any excess thinner off onto a tissue. Then apply the filter sparingly over the model, taking care not to flood the model as a subtle effect is desired.

Step 8. Paint the wheels with dark grey. Never use black because this is too harsh. Paint the tracks dark brown. Then paint the guns dark grey and, once dry, lightly brush over with gunmetal. Then paint the tools and any stowage in the appropriate colours: it is best to keep these muted, because if the colours are too bright they will detract from the overall finish.

Step 9. Now apply any decals. None are provided with this kit, but water slide decals are easy to use and can be bought from several suppliers. Two products that assist in the application of water slide decals are Micro Sol and Micro Set. Micro Sol softens decals before application, which makes them easier to conform to uneven surfaces. Micro Set, when brushed onto the desired location of the decal on the model, will provide good adhesion. To apply,

LEFT AND BELOW: Paint the wheels, guns, tools and any stowage.

remove the decal from the sheet and dip it into the warm water just to dampen it. Dab lightly with a tissue to remove any excess fluid. Then apply the decal in the chosen position with the aid of a soft brush. Once done, leave to dry, and then apply an even coat of matt varnish. After leaving it to dry for at least twenty-four hours, another coat of matt varnish should be applied to protect it.

Step 10. Next weather the model, following the steps given for the Sherman Jumbo (*see* Chapter 6). Use MIG P232 'Dry Mud' for the lower areas and P037 'Gulf War Sand' for the upper surfaces.

The finished model with decals and weathering.

M2 HALF-TRACK

The M2 and M3 were first put out to tender in late 1940 and a contract to produce 424 vehicles was awarded to the Autocar company, which had its factory located in Ardmore, Pennsylvania. The Diamond T Company of Chicago was given a contract to produce the M3, and the White Motor Company, which was already producing the M2A1 scout car, was added to the list of companies producing the M3 and M2 half-track. Some 13,500 M2s were produced by the White Motor Company alone.

The first M2s were deployed in 1941. In North Africa from early 1942 they were issued to artillery units for use as both an ammunition carrier and a prime mover for the 105mm Howitzer. The M2 was also issued to infantry units to carry machine gun squads and for reconnaissance units. The other use of the M2 was as a prime mover for the 57mm Anti-Tank gun, the role that will be modelled here using a Plastic Soldier Company (PSC) M3 Half-track with the addition of an S&S Models M2 resin conversion rear body, which was designed to fit with the Plastic Soldier Company M3.

The S&S resin replacement body next to the PSC M3 part, part of which it will replace.

Use either a Dremel or a razor saw to cut the plastic. When using a power tool on plastic be aware that the plastic will soften during the cutting process.

Modelling the M2 Half-Track

Step 1. Start by carefully marking the area behind the driving compartment that needs to be removed to fit the new resin body. Use either a Dremel or a razor saw. When using any power tool on plastic, take into account that the plastic will soften during the cutting process due to friction, so the cut should be made several millimetres from the actual mark made. Next, with great care, make another cut behind the driving compartment to remove more of the unwanted plastic, then carefully remove the last pieces with a sharp knife. Throughout this process keep fitting the two pieces together until a good fit is achieved.

Step 2. Now fit the rear chassis: in order to achieve a snug fit, the two pieces at the end will need to be removed. Then glue it to the underside of the resin

ABOVE LEFT: This stage will take great accuracy when cutting. The advice is 'measure twice, cut once'.

ABOVE RIGHT: The two pieces of the PSC kit that must be cut away from the sub-frame. Doing this will allow this piece to fit snugly to the S&S body.

LEFT: The chassis is now fitted to the replacement conversion body.

superstructure using cyanoacrylate. Glue the new resin body to the front and leave it supported for an hour to allow the glue to dry. When this is complete the joint between the new resin body and the cab of the half-track may need some minor filling.

ABOVE: Some stowage has been added.

Step 3. Attach the track units and axle and wheels. Leave the driver's compartment open, as this will need to be painted before proceeding further: it will be a challenge to paint once the M2 is fully built. Paint the driver and co-driver following the instructions provided for painting infantry as the uniforms were similar (*see* Chapter 3).

BELOW: The PSC M3 half-track has now been converted into an M2 half-track.

Step 4. The build can now be completed by fitting the bonnet, the stowage racks and some stowage. The .30 calibre machine gun that is added to the model comes with the PSC kit. Use grey primer, then paint and weather as for the other vehicles covered in this chapter, especially the M15, as the colours and technique are the same.

The completed model with passengers, towing a 57mm Anti-Tank gun.

US TANK CREW UNIFORMS

The uniforms worn by US tank crews changed little between 1942 and 1945. The M-1938 tanker helmet was similar to those then worn by American footballers. From the mid-1930s it became clear that tank crews should be issued with appropriate head protection against knocks and bangs from the inside the tank, especially when moving cross-country at speed. A patent for the helmet submitted on 1 May 1941 referred to it as the M-1938, pertaining to the year when the design developed.

The M-1938 tanker helmet was issued to all tank crews from 1942 onwards. It offered first-class protection and was comfortable to wear, and so was a popular item of kit. Even Military Police were seen wearing it while riding motorcycles. It has to be noted that this helmet was purely designed to protect the wearer from knocks and bumps, just like a motorcycle crash helmet, and it was not designed to protect from ballistics.

Just like the infantry, tank crews wore a mix of M-1941 jackets, HBT overalls and standard boots. In winter and cold climates, crews also wore winter combat trousers, which came up to the chest.

The Milicast set has a good variety of uniforms and the figures look relaxed. One crewman even has a Thompson sub-machine gun.

Modelling US tank crew

These figures are from one of the sets offered by Milicast in 1:76 scale and they depict the style of dress worn by tank crews from 1942 to 1945. The set is cast in high-quality resin, designed to complement the various US armour kits in the Milicast range.

Step 1. Prepare the figures for painting by cleaning away any mould lines and flash with a file and sharp knife. Then mount them on a piece of card or similar with the aid of glue. In this example, the figures are on sprues and will be painted in situ. First paint with black primer and leave to dry (about an hour in a warm room).

Step 2. Start by applying a base coat of AK3071 'Dark Olive Green/M-43 Uniform Green Olive'. Even though this colour is intended for a later uniform, it will be fine for the HBT overalls worn by tank crews. Then add some white and use the mixture to apply highlights. Paint the M-1941 jackets with AK3075 'US Field Drab'. Add the base colour 'Red Brown' for the areas of flesh.

Step 3. Add white paint to the colours used in step 2 and add highlights to the painted areas. Then paint

The base colours of the uniforms applied.

The base colours of the jackets and overalls have been highlighted.

the areas of flesh using the technique described in Chapter 3. Now paint the belts with AK3074 'Brown Olive Drab' and highlight as before: this colour works very well when painting US Army webbing. The M-1938 helmet is also painted with 'Brown Olive Drab' and highlighted as for the uniform. The helmet had leather edges on the ear flaps, so paint these as well.

Step 4. Next, paint the boots, goggles and holsters – tank crewmen were issued with hand guns – using a very dark grey. Paint the goggles' strap with Vallejo 924 'Russian Uniform' and edge the goggles with this colour too. With a fine brush paint the goggles' lens in gunmetal. Finally, apply a dark brown diluted wash and leave to dry before applying two coats of matt varnish.

LEFT: Further details have been added.

BELOW: The completed figures prior to construction.

Normandy 5

ON 6 JUNE 1944 the forces of the Allied nations launched an invasion along an 80km (50 mile) stretch of the Normandy coast divided into five beaches. This was codenamed Operation *Neptune* but became more widely known as D-Day.

Prior to the assault from the sea, three parachute divisions were dropped behind the coast of Normandy. These were the British 6th Airborne Division, which landed in the Orne basin near Ranville to secure the Allied left flank, the 82nd 'All American' and the 101st 'Screaming Eagles' Division. The two American divisions landed behind the American beaches and were tasked with securing a number of bridges and towns to prevent the Germans sending reinforcements to the beach defenders, as well as launching counter-attacks directly onto the beaches. The American drops into Normandy, however, did not go as well as those of their British counterparts. Both divisions had units that were either lost or became mixed up with other units when pilots mistook drop zones or tried to avoid heavy anti-aircraft fire.

The Germans had also flooded large areas behind the coast and many were dropped into sometimes quite deep water. Weighed down by their heavy kit, some sadly drowned. Nevertheless, these elite soldiers soon grouped together and, despite depleted numbers, they achieved their assigned objectives, even defeating much larger enemy units in the process.

The assault beaches on D-Day were codenamed Sword, Gold, Juno, Omaha and Utah. Omaha and Utah were designated for the Americans. The landings on Omaha were in doubt until quite late in the day due to very strong German resistance, which caused large casualties to the first waves of assaulting infantry. The units that assaulted Omaha

Willys supply Jeep of the 82nd Airborne Division, Normandy, June 1944.

were the 29th Infantry Division and 1st 'Big Red One' Infantry Division, as well as nine companies of Rangers. H hour was set at 06.30 hours and the casualties in the first wave were horrendous. The second fared little better, but at 07.35 small groups of American Infantry and Rangers started to find gaps in the defences. At Draw F1 at Fox Green Beach, near Vierville, the 3rd Battalion of Grenadier Regiment 725 reported that up to 200 American infantrymen from Regimental Combat Team 116 of the 29th Infantry Division had penetrated the German defences. While this was going on, companies A and B of the 2nd Rangers, led by Lieutenant Colonel James Rudder, attacked Pointe du Hoc where the 155mm battery posed a serious danger to the landings at Omaha some 5km (3 miles) away. This assault was made famous through the 1962 film *The Longest Day*. The 5th Ranger Battalion was also intended to support this assault, but after a 40-minute delay this unit was diverted to Omaha to help with the landings there. Had it not done so more casualties would have resulted.

The assault forces that attacked Pointe du Hoc lost half their number to German fire on the run in to the beach. They were landed by British landing craft and used 100ft ladders requisitioned from the London Fire Brigade to scale the cliffs. Cover was provided by fire from two destroyers, USS *Satterlee* and HMS *Talybont*, which kept the German defenders from the cliff tops as the Rangers made their climb. They soon found that the ladders were short but they persevered and made their way to the top. There they carried out the assault on the concrete emplacements, only to find that the guns had been moved. They were later found and put out of action a few miles from Pointe du Hoc by a patrol of Rangers. This action was one of the most daring carried out on D-Day and was the scene of extreme bravery both during and after the assault as the Germans launched a series of counter-attacks.

At the same time, some sixteen teams of engineers were being landed in areas where there were no soldiers or tanks to provide cover, and they set about clearing beach obstacles and looking for mines while under heavy fire in order to make the beach safe for the following waves of soldiers and vehicles. These men showed extreme bravery and steadfastness to duty under very difficult conditions as they helped to ensure the success of the landings on 6 June 1944.

After the landings, the Allies drove inland across wide open fields, near Caen in the British Sector, that provided fine 'tank country'. In the central sector, however, the landscape was marked by the bocage field system, in which the sides of the fields are often

M16 anti-aircraft half-track in Normandy, June 1944.

ABOVE: US Airborne troops in Normandy, 8 June 1944.

RIGHT: A Sherman tank fitted with a Culin prong leads the way through the Normandy bocage.

made from hedges 2 metres thick set on banks mixed with mature trees, which had developed over centuries. The medieval hedges were a defender's paradise and an attacker's hell: the two sides slugged it out field by field for days or even weeks, sometimes changing hands as many as three times a day. Among the problems the American and other Allied armies faced in Normandy was how best to deal with the bocage, employing infantry to operate in close coordination with the armoured forces to prevent ambushes, which were commonplace given the numerous places for concealment.

The Panzerfaust was an inexpensive, but much-feared, one-shot anti-tank rocket that could take out any Allied tank with a single shot. The firer could then move to another position, pick up a second Panzerfaust and lie in wait for another tank to come within the 60m range. It was difficult for tanks, even a

Sherman, to move directly through a bocage hedge as this exposed the thin armour on the belly of the tank, presenting an easy target for a Panzerfaust. Many tanks were lost in this way.

Sergeant Curtis G. Culin, however, after a conversation with a fellow tanker called 'Roberts', both of the 2nd Armored Division and from Tennessee, came up with the idea of fitting knives to the front of a tank that would then cut through the banks and hedges. This allowed tanks to drive through, rather than over, the bocage and turned the Sherman into a bulldozer/hedge cutter, while protecting the underside of the tank from attack. A prototype made from scrap iron was shown to General Omar Bradley, who was so impressed that he ordered it to be fitted to as many tanks as possible for the upcoming Operation *Cobra*, which was to enable the breakout from the Normandy bocage. Up to 60 per cent of the tanks were then fitted with the so-called 'Culin prong', which aided the American breakout in late July.

US INFANTRY

This chapter deals with the GI as he appeared both on D-Day and during the fighting in Normandy until the breakout in late July. Infantry, Engineers and paratroopers, as well as the uniforms they wore, will be covered here together with a variety of armoured vehicles.

Painting US Infantry

This 20mm metal figure of an officer from June 1944, produced by AB Miniatures, provides an example of the uniform worn by the infantry. He will be painted wearing regulation uniform as used in Normandy,

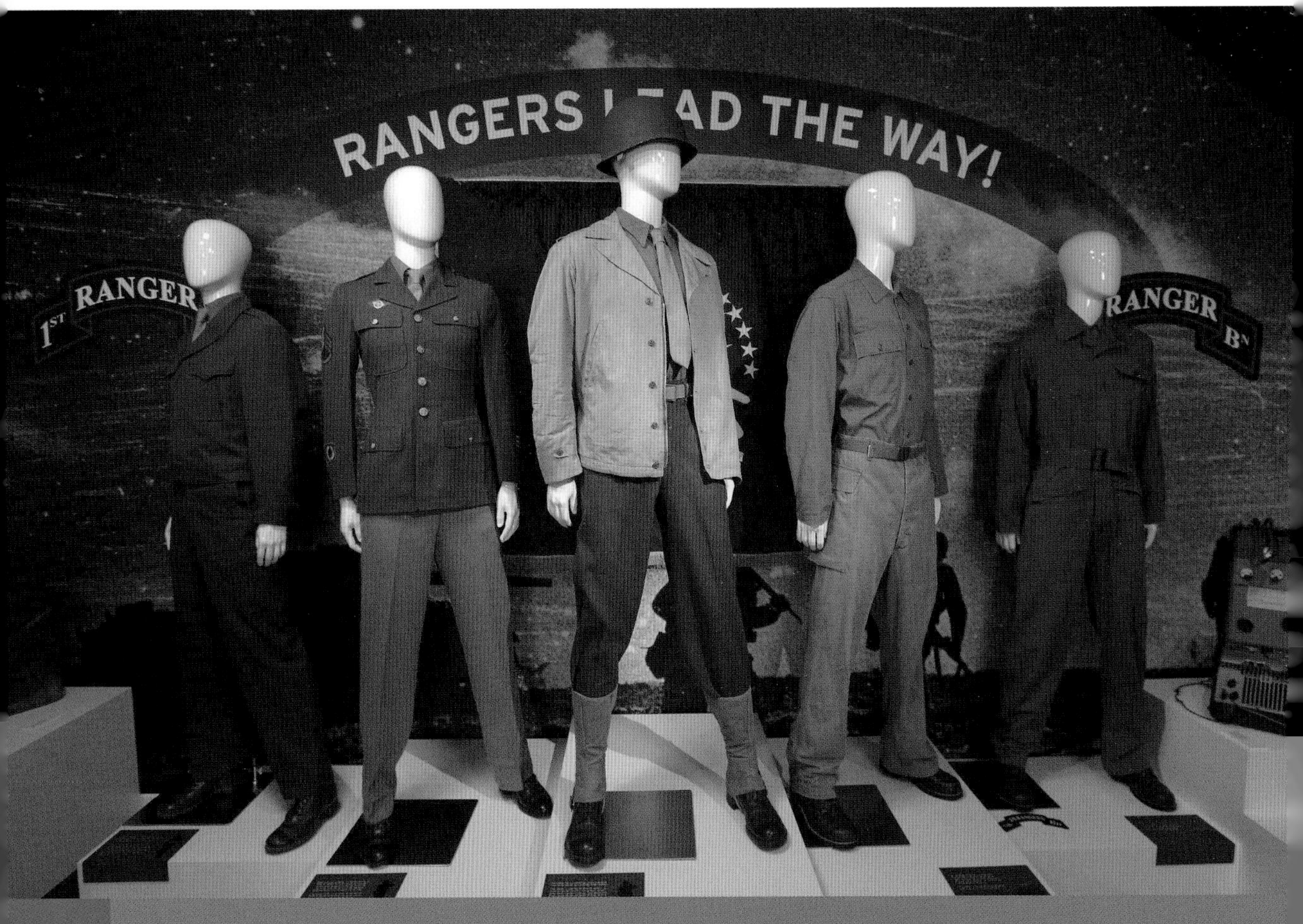

This photo shows actual WWII uniforms worn by the GI in Europe from 1944 to 1945.

the M1941 jacket and the M1938 woollen trousers, as seen in films such as *Saving Private Ryan*.

Step 1. Check for any mould lines and clean them. Attach the figure to a base (here a 20mm round base has been used) and then prime the figure. When this is dry the figure is ready to paint.

Step 2. Paint the jacket using AK3075 'US Field Drab'. When this is dry, lighten the paint by adding a little Vallejo 819 'Iraqi Sand' and gently paint over the raised areas.

Step 3. The trousers should be painted in Vallejo 921 'English Uniform'. When dry, mix the paint with a little 'Iraqi Sand' to make a highlighter and apply to the raised areas. Do not overwork the effect as in reality the trousers should still look darker than the jacket.

Step 4. Now paint the flesh areas as described in Chapter 3. The weapon, which in this case is a Thompson sub-machine gun, is next: start with black, and then brush over with dark grey. Gunmetal is not actually silver but a black/blue colour. Then paint the wooden parts with Vallejo 311 'New Wood' as the base, and lightened with a little white for a highlight. Then paint the straps and any webbing with AK3076 'Canvas Tone' from the AK US Army paint set. Highlight these with the same colour, but with a little white added. Now paint the boots a red-brown colour: Vallejo 846 'Mahogany Brown' is a good choice.

Step 5. Now attend to the other details, such as the bayonet. Even officers carried a bayonet, which could be used as a fighting knife during close combat. This should be painted as for the weapons, as they had metal scabbards with wooden hand grips. Now highlight the jackets and belts again, using the same colours as before, but add a little more white paint to achieve a balanced effect. Also paint the buttons and caps on the top of the canteens in gunmetal. Once the painting and highlighting on the uniform is satisfactory, paint the divisional insignia on the left shoulder of the figure. This officer has been given one from the 29th Infantry Division, which landed on Omaha beach on D-Day. The figure should now be matt varnished for protection.

The basic uniform has been painted and a start made on the flesh areas.

The figure's uniform and equipment are now complete.

The shoulder flash of the 29th Infantry Division, also known as the 'Blue and Grey', which landed on Omaha beach and fought its way throughout the Normandy campaign, finally reaching Bremen at the end of the war.

The division's 116th Regiment was attached to the 1st Infantry Division, 'The Big Red One', and was in the first assault wave on D-Day.

The completed officer.

LEFT: The set of 1:35 scale figures from which a Ranger will be chosen to paint as an example.

BELOW: Attach the model to a temporary base and fill any gaps using Green Stuff.

THE RANGER ON D-DAY

At the time of writing there were no 20mm or 28mm WWII Rangers models of sufficient quality to use for a painting demonstration. Instead, the 1:35 scale Dragon set of Rangers has been used. These are similar to the 1:32 scale American infantryman on Okinawa (*see* Chapter 2) and are also multi-part figures. They are superbly detailed and illustrate Rangers very well. They also wear the Assault Vest, modelled on the British battle jerkin, as used on D-Day by specialist assault troops such as combat engineers and Rangers. Soldiers liked the vest as there were several useful pockets to hold equipment and ammunition. The vests were replaced after D-Day in favour of standard webbing.

The demonstration model will also carry a Bangalore torpedo section, which was used to clear wire obstacles by joining together metal tubes filled with explosives that could then be detonated. A famous scene in *Saving Private Ryan* shows a Bangalore torpedo being used to clear the wire and open up a way off the beach for Tom Hanks and his men.

Painting the Ranger on D-Day

The Dragon kit comes with all that is needed to construct five Rangers.

Step 1. Start by constructing the body and arms: any small gaps between the parts may be filled with Green Stuff putty. Although some of these may subsequently be covered by equipment, never leave anything to chance.

Step 2. Next add the equipment, following the instructions, and then the head and helmet. Make sure they are all correctly fitted. The instructions provided are good but check against photo references to ensure accuracy. Add a rifle sling made from thin paper glued in the correct position. Bases are not supplied with the kit, these should be added.

ABOVE LEFT: More gaps filled with Green Stuff.

ABOVE RIGHT: The primed figure is ready to be painted and is now on a permanent base.

RIGHT: Start by applying the relevant base colours for the uniform.

Step 3. Prime the figure. This figure wears the assault vest and the M-1943 HBT trousers, which had large pockets on both sides that were useful for carrying equipment such as explosives. Base coat the assault vest with Vallejo 924 'Russian Uniform', then paint with AK3076 'Canvas Tone', and finally lighten some 'Canvas Tone' with a little white and use this for the highlights.

Step 4. Paint the jacket with AK3075 'US Field Drab'. Once this base coat is dry, add a little white to the paint and start to highlight. Repeat the process until a pleasing result, not too light in colour, is achieved.

Step 5. Base coat the trousers with Vallejo 921 'English Uniform'. Then highlight these with the 'US Field Drab' and 'English Uniform' mixed 50:50. M-1943 HBT trousers were a dark olive colour, so use AK3071 'Dark Olive Green/M-43 Uniform Green Olive', diluted with water at a ratio of 7:3. If the first coat is not enough, apply another. The work already done will help to soften the effect of the olive paint, and the thinned paint will gather in the creases and give a pleasing shaded effect.

Once the base colours have been applied, the model is allowed to dry.

Paint the gaiters, boots, rifle and sling.
Then paint the hands and face.

Step 6. Paint the gaiters with 'US Field Drab' and the boots, rifle and sling with AK3073 'Red Brown Leather'. Paint the hands and face as well, following the instructions given for the GI in Chapter 2.

Step 7. Paint the helmet with Vallejo 889 'Olive Brown'. Then paint the spade handle and the wooden parts of the gun with Vallejo 311 'New Wood'. The Bangalore torpedo section is painted 'Olive Brown'. Mix some gunmetal paint with just a little black and paint any buttons on the assault vest as well as the buttons on the gaiters. Paint the bayonet's scabbard 'Brown Olive'. The chinstrap is painted using 'Canvas Tone', and the strap at the front peak of the helmet, which holds the metal helmet shell onto the helmet liner, is painted 'Red Brown Leather'. Leave the figure to dry for a hour, then wash the uniform with dark brown ink, thinned 50/50 with acrylic thinner. Then leave to dry before matt coating and finally basing.

Paint in the insignia. The Ranger badge goes on the left shoulder. The orange Ranger patch is painted on the rear of the helmet.

The painted Ranger on its completed base. Apply some dry sand and paint it with MIG 'Beach Sand', working it into the surface to create a realistic finish.

US COMBAT ENGINEERS

These soldiers played a prominent and important role during the Normandy campaign assisting the advance of the US Army through the Normandy bocage. They cleared obstacles from the beaches and made safe the various mines and booby traps left behind by German forces. This model shows a mine-clearing team of six men, with a Sergeant in command equipped with two mine detectors. The other members of the team are searching for mines with a bayonet, a practice widely used by infantry and taught as part of their training, and carrying away a German Teller mine. The NCO is giving instructions to search for more.

Painting US Combat Engineers

Step 1. Engineers and their officers, for the most part, wore the same dress as the infantry (*see* above). Any webbing and backpacks should be painted with AK3076 'Canvas Tone', and then a lighter tone with some white added should be used for highlighting.

Step 2. The equipment carried by combat engineers was largely the same as that issued to the infantry. Follow the steps outlined above for painting the 29th Infantry Division officer. The mine detectors are painted Vallejo 887 'Brown Violet' and highlighted with this paint to which a little white has been added. Again, these are painted as belonging to the 29th Infantry Division, so paint as before, including the NCO who is a Sergeant. Finish by basing the model, as described in Chapter 8.

THE US PARATROOPER ON D-DAY

On the evening of D-Day, some 13,000 paratroopers of the two American airborne divisions, the 82nd and 101st, boarded their aircraft and set out for Normandy. For many it would be their first time in combat, while others, especially those of the 82nd Airborne who had fought in Sicily, were no less uncertain as what would happen when they landed in enemy-occupied France. The full story of what followed the landings may be found elsewhere, but their impact was to confuse the German forces and help the seaborne forces get inland.

A US Paratrooper on D-Day would have worn the M-1942-type uniform, the design of which was developed by Captain William P. Yarborough, Test Officer of the Provisional Parachute Group. The M-1942 Jump Uniform consisted of trousers and jacket made from a tan lightweight cotton material. The jacket had a zip on the front as well as four large pockets; the back had bi-swing pleats. A belt was also sewn into the jacket. The trousers had two large thigh pockets. The uniform gave little protection from the weather, unlike the later M-1943 olive drab jacket and trousers (*see* Chapter 6).

Modelling the US Paratrooper on D-Day

This is an Elhiem 20mm Paratrooper in authentic colours to represent a US Paratrooper as he looked during D-Day and in the subsequent fighting in Normandy in June 1944. Elhiem make a specific

A group of US combat engineers undertaking mine detection and clearance.

range of US airborne figures for the Normandy campaign and the detail is first class.

Step 1. Inspect the figures for mould lines and blemishes and remove them with a file and sharp craft knife. Then mount the figures, in this case on to round 20mm bases. Once the superglue is cured, paint PVA glue onto the bases and around the figures' feet, and then sprinkle on dried builders' sand and leave to dry. Once dry, prime the figures using grey car primer.

Step 2. Now paint the entire figure with the authentic tan colour for the M-1942 uniform. Add a little white to the base colour and brush this over the earlier coat, which will help with the final finish of the uniform.

LEFT: A unit of Engineers equipped for mine clearance. These 20mm figures from AB Miniatures have been primed and base coated, ready for the next stage.

BELOW: The base painting is now complete.

Step 3. Paint the webbing and backpacks with Vallejo 924 'Russian Uniform'. The weapons should be painted with dark brown. Paint the faces and boots with Vallejo 818 'Red Leather'. Doing this now will help speed up the process of painting the figures.

Step 4. Using AK3076 'Canvas Tone', paint the webbing again, but leave some of the base colour showing through at creases and joints, as this helps create shade. Paint the faces and hands as previously laid out, going from dark to light and leaving a little of the previous shade so that it creates depth as well as interest to the face and hands.

Step 5. Next paint the weapons: first the metal parts with a dark gunmetal, then the wooden parts using Vallejo 311 'New Wood', then add white to this and carefully highlight the wooden parts, but do not overdo this stage. These Elhiem figures were designed for use in D-Day and as such wear the M-1942 uniform with olive reinforcing patches on the knees: paint these with 'Russian Uniform'.

RIGHT: After the uniforms and equipment have been highlighted, and the areas of flesh completed, the figures are nearly ready.

BELOW: The knee and elbow patches, which were added to protect the suit from wear, have been painted with Vallejo 'Russian Uniform' and the figures are ready for the dark brown wash.

The completed figures, all based and ready to game with.

Step 6. Apply a dark brown wash over the entire figure. When this dries it will pick out creases and other details that otherwise would be hard to see on such a small figure. The wash will also help everything that has been painted to blend in and give a more 'on campaign' look, rather than an overly bright finish. Once dry, coat the figures with a good matt varnish for protection and then complete the bases.

M10 TANK DESTROYER

The M10 Tank Destroyer came into being when the US Army saw the need for a fully tracked tank destroyer with a rotating turret that would give improved manoeuvrability (the T12 half-track was lacking in both requirements). The prototype was produced in early 1942. After some changes the 3-inch Motor Carriage M10 went into production in

This 1:72 scale M10 from the author's collection is based on a commercially available ready-painted model. A lot of stowage has been added and the model repainted.

June 1943. The M10 was based on the modified hull of a M4A2 Sherman and mounted a 3-inch M7 gun in an open turret. M10s based on the M4A3 were designated M10A1. General Motors' Fisher Arsenal in Michigan produced some 4,993 M10s and 375 M10A1s from September 1942 to December 1943.

The M10 tank destroyers were first deployed in small numbers in Tunisia in 1943. The crews liked them as they allowed good all-round visibility, which is vital in armoured warfare, and they were easier to escape from when disabled than the Shermans. The M10 was still in use during 1945, even after it had been superseded by the M18 Hellcat and the M36 Jackson.

Modelling the M10 Tank Destroyer

There are a few detailed kits of the M10. The Ukrainian company UM Models (Uni-Model) produces kits of both the early and late (Wolverine) versions, but at the time of writing these are getting hard to find. The Armourfast kit is the only option for a plastic model. Although it lacks a lot of detail, this can be overcome to a large extent by using aftermarket add-on sets, such as those used with the M35 Jackson (*see* Chapter 7). There are also resin kits of the M10 produced by Milicast and metal kits by SHQ Miniatures of a similar type to the M15 featured in Chapter 4.

M4 SHERMAN THUNDERBOLT IV AND CREIGHTON ABRAMS

The M4 Sherman modelled here is one of the best-known tank commanders' tanks from WWII. It was used by Lt Col Creighton Abrams Jr, who was in command of the 4th Armored Division's 37th Tank Battalion, the motto of which was 'Courage Conquers'. He used his tanks to great advantage by leveraging their speed and reliability, taking on the better-armed and armoured Panzers and coming out on top. He always led from the front and could be found at the toughest part of a battle. He also cared about the wellbeing of his men. General Patton called him the best tank commander in WWII after only himself, which was high praise indeed.

Modelling the M4 Sherman Thunderbolt IV

The Milicast kit chosen here is an M4 Sherman of the type used by Creighton Abrams in France in August 1944. The decals are from an Aleran Miniatures set of 'US Sherman Aces', which has markings for several well-known Shermans.

Step 1. As always, lay out the parts as it helps to identify them and where they go. These simple kits

The kit as it comes from Milicast.

LEFT: The new stowage has been added.

BELOW: Paint the model with acrylic MIG 'Olive Drab'.

seldom come with plans, so a good reference source will help. Next, build the kit and decide whether to leave the commander's hatch open, as was done with this model. Add a little stowage to the rear deck, if desired. Once built, wash in mild detergent and warm water and leave to dry, ready for painting.

Step 2. The Thunderbolt IV had a .50 calibre heavy machine gun, and this needs to be added to the commander's hatch from the spares box. It is better to add this now, rather than earlier, because delicate details could be damaged when the model is cleaned. The model may now be primed with grey car paint.

Step 3. Using an airbrush, paint the model with acrylic MIG 926 'Olive Drab'. Follow the steps described previously for the M15 Anti-aircraft Half-track (*see* Chapter 4).

Step 4. Weather this model with MIG P232 'Dry Mud' and P028 'Europe Dust' for the upper areas.

The completed model.

THE CULIN PRONG 'HEDGE CUTTER'

The Culin prong came in several forms as no set pattern ever existed for it. The first examples were constructed from girders taken from beach defences and cut with the aid of a blowtorch into pieces that, when assembled and fitted to the front of a tank, created forked prongs. These were a feature of American tanks but were also used by British tanks in Normandy from July 1944.

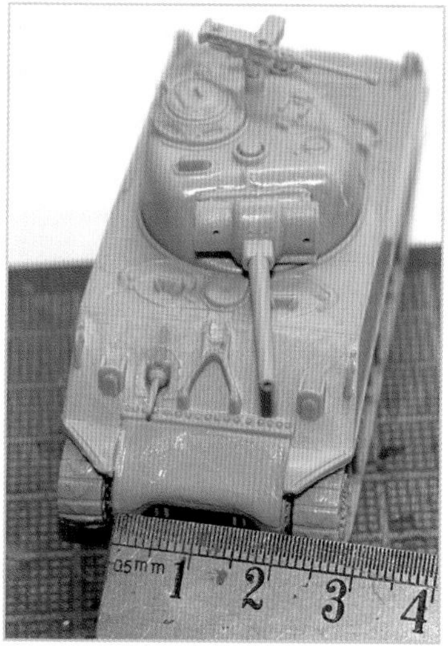

LEFT: Measure between the tracks.

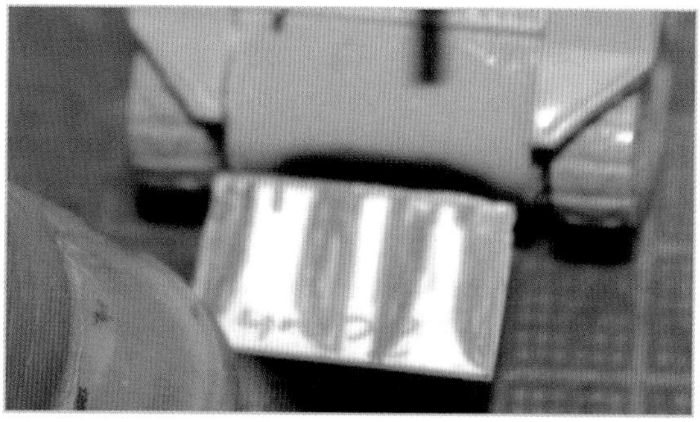

BELOW: The teeth have been marked out.

Modelling the Culin Prong 'Hedge Cutter'

This project will need 39 thou plasticard, a ruler, sharp knife, a fine file and a pencil. Measure the distance between the tracks on the front of the model. This is an Italeri 1:72 scale M4A3 Sherman and the distance is 20mm. Mark out a rectangle on the card measuring 20 × 12mm and draw the shape of the actual cutters onto this with a pencil. Match this up to the area between the track to check that the marked teeth look good and are neatly distanced apart.

Cut them out and then mark out another set using these original teeth as a guide. When all the prongs are cut out, file them to shape so that both sets are the same. Align them and glue them together so that only four teeth are showing.

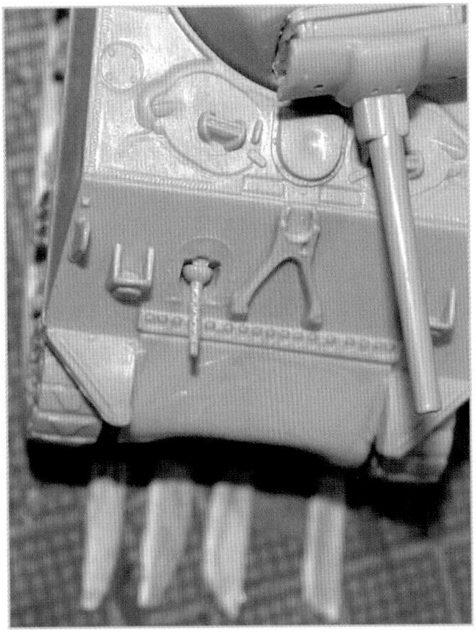

Place the teeth in front of the model as shown and check the spacing of each one.

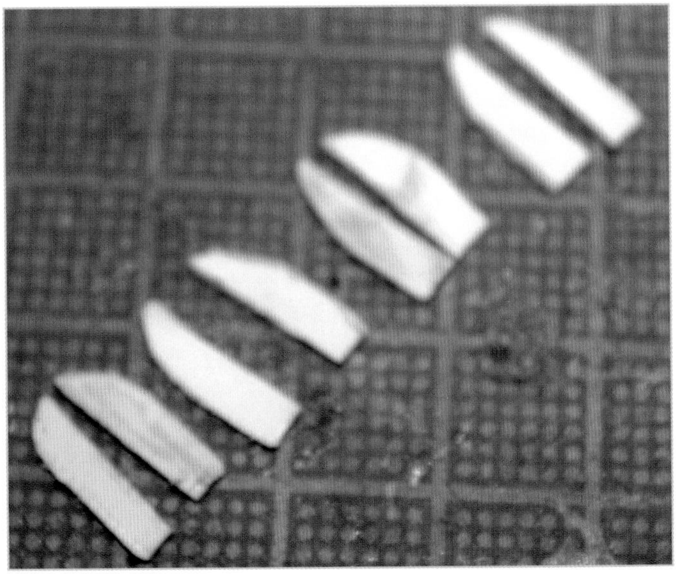

Both sets should be the mirror image of the other. Use a fine file to remove any excess plastic.

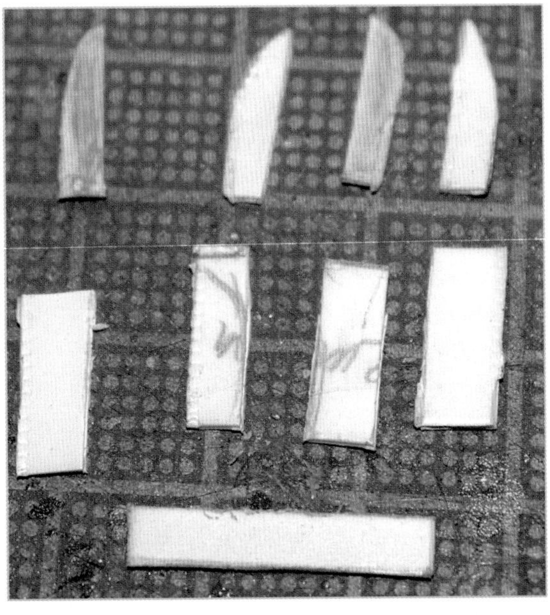

LEFT: Note how the teeth should be placed and assembled along with the back piece.

RIGHT: The prong being assembled.

BELOW: Once glued to the Sherman, the prong is ready for some paint.

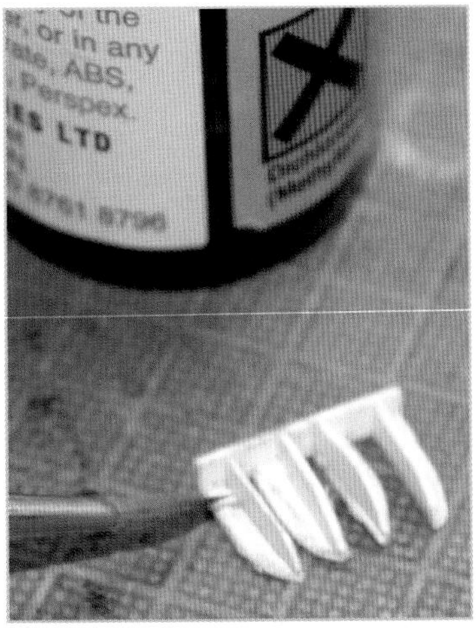

To create the rear of the prong, measure a piece of card 20 × 4mm and cut it out. Attach the four teeth to it with glue. Start with the two outside teeth and work into the two inner teeth.

Fit this to the Sherman with some liquid polystyrene cement.

The Seine to the Bulge, 25 August 1944–January 1945 6

AFTER THE BREAKOUT FROM Normandy at the end of July 1944, the German 7th Army was in full retreat towards Germany when it became trapped in the Falaise pocket and was mostly destroyed by late August 1944. Those German units that did manage to break out were pressed every step of the way by Allied air and ground forces. Among these was the 3rd Army, led by George S. Patton Jr, a commander who pushed his men hard but achieved results that few could match. The Allies had yet to secure a fully working port from which to supply their armies. Their fast advance and the even faster retreat of German forces meant that the Allies were starting to run low on vital supplies, notably fuel. In late August 1944 the Allies slowed their pursuit of the retreating German units, which in turn, gave them precious time to rest, reform, re-equip and wait for the next Allied move.

The stage was set for one of the momentous campaigns of WWII, Operation *Market Garden*, which took place from 17 to 25 September 1944. This

Stalking a Panther, the Netherlands, 1944.

M18 Hellcat on the road to
Arracourt, September 1945.

General George S. Patton Jr.

A Jeep patrol ahead of the main
advance in France, late August 1944.

Using a captured German Kübelwagen,
this US officer scans for the enemy.

operation saw the use of two US Airborne Divisions (the 101st 'Screaming Eagles' and the 82nd 'All American'), the British 1st Airborne Division together with the Polish 1st Independent Parachute Brigade. The objective was to secure a series of bridges that would eventually lead the Allies into Germany thus, hopefully, shortening the war. Unfortunately, the goal of reaching the final bridge at Arnhem was not achieved by the British XXX Corps in the face of strong German opposition.

As this period is so synonymous with the airborne soldier this chapter will focus on how to model and paint the American Paratrooper as he looked during both Operation *Market Garden* and the Battle of the Bulge (16 December 1944 – 25 January 1945), which was marked by the 101st Airborne Division's defence of the Belgian town of Bastogne. The uniform worn at this time by American Paratroopers was the M-1943, a much greener hue (olive drab) than the tan colour of the earlier M-1942 uniform used in Normandy, although many veterans chose to keep their M-1942 uniforms as a mark of their veteran status. The replacement of the red leather Corcoran jump boots by combat boots was fiercely resisted by the Airborne for reasons that were related to both status and safety: the jump boot was seen as the mark of a trained paratrooper, signifying his elite status above the regular infantry, while the combat boot had a buckle that could snag on the static line and cause serious injury or even death.

PAINTING A LARGE 20MM WARGAMES UNIT

This example demonstrates how to paint a larger number of figures, which is a useful technique to learn when building up an army for wargaming. There are times when a gamer needs to get a unit painted quickly, but does not really have the time to paint the figures to a standard requiring a lot of shading and detailing.

The figures are 20mm metal miniatures manufactured by TQD Castings and represent a platoon of Paratroopers in the M-1943 uniform as worn during Operation *Market Garden*.

Step 1. Always check over each figure for mould lines and flash, and remove this with the aid of a fine file and a sharp craft knife. This step must always be carried out and should never be skipped. Once this is done, attach the figures to their bases using cyanoacrylate glue. In this case the figures come with plastic slotta bases, which have a slot that accepts the corresponding locating bar moulded to the figure's feet. Prime the figures using a light grey primer and then leave to dry.

Step 2. When painting larger numbers of figures, paint only ten figures at a time, which makes it possible to get through them without undue fatigue. The sight of the unit growing quickly will help inspire

The unit has been base coated with thinned AK3071 'Dark Olive Green/M-43 Uniform Green Olive'. Note the variation in shade, which will add interest to the unit when completed.

tackling another ten figures and so on. Start by applying a coat of AK3071 'Dark Olive Green/M-43 Uniform Green Olive' thinned down at a ratio of 2:1 paint to thinner. Thinning the paint allows it to flow freely over the figure and helps to create basic highlighting and shading. It is always better to use a lighter tone with smaller figures. Then leave to dry thoroughly.

Step 3. Paint the webbing using a thin 000 brush and AK 3076 'Canvas Tone'. When dry, highlight with the same colour mixed 2:1 with Vallejo 819 'Iraqi Sand'. While this is drying paint the faces with Vallejo 955 'Flat Flesh'. Then once dry, paint over with 'Flat Flesh' mixed with a little white. Paint the helmet with AK3074 'Brown Olive Drab'.

With Vallejo 846 'Mahogany Brown', paint the boots and wooden parts, such as the rifle and entrenching tools. When dry, highlight the entrenching tool and rifles using Vallejo 311 'New Wood'. Leave to dry.

Step 4. Wash over the figures with thinned sepia ink diluted 2:1 with water. This wash will help to bring out the detail, especially on the webbing. Leave to dry for a few hours in a warm room. Once dry, give the figures a coat of matt varnish and add a base when dry.

Do not paint more than ten figures at a time. This method can be used to complete a unit quickly as the large numbers mean that a lot can be done without long gaps between the stages once the main colours have dried, and in this case the uniforms were of one colour.

The figures with the details painted. They will need a colour wash and an optional coat of matt varnish to finish them off.

Seven 'Screaming Eagles', September 1944.

The entire unit of 36 figures painted and based.

Men from the 82nd Airborne move cautiously past abandoned German vehicles. They wear the M-1942 style uniform.

M4A3E2 SHERMAN 'JUMBO'

In early 1944 the US Army needed an assault tank for the upcoming campaign in Europe. The T26E1, or Pershing as it became later, would not be ready in time so they considered how they could produce an armoured version of the M4 Sherman to fulfil the role in the short term.

The original idea for upgrading the M4 Sherman actually came from the British, who in 1941 asked for a more heavily armoured M4, which was about to be cast. This was considered but did not work. The US War Department, however, did not forget this suggestion and in December 1943 General Motors were asked to test an M4 with additional weight added. After some 500 miles of testing, the tank's performance was found to suffer very little.

In March 1944 the Ordnance Department made a deal that 254 M4 Shermans would be up-armoured. The new design was designated M4A3E2 (the 'E' stood for experimental design). Production was stepped up and by late 1944 the vehicles were being delivered to tank crews in Europe. The turret was of a new design based on the T23 76 turret, which now had 6in of armour, compared to only 3in at the thickest part on the standard M4 turret. The armour was much improved with an extra inch to the front. The new tank was fitted with a 75mm main gun, but in the field this was sometimes changed to a 76mm, due mainly to the 75mm gun's proven characteristics when firing HE.

About 100 M4s were modified in the field with additional armour and known as 'Expedient Jumbos'. Creighton Abrams (*see* Chapter 5) used one of these Thunderbolt VIIs in 1945.

Jumbos were used as break-through tanks when attacking fortifications and as column leaders. They were able to withstand being hit and this exposed the German anti-tank gun or tank to fire from the rest of the column.

Modelling the M4A3E2 Sherman 'Jumbo'

One of the Jumbos used during the Battle of the Bulge was 'Cobra King', which belonged to the 37th Tank Battalion of the 4th Armored Division. This Milicast kit is in resin, and as such there is not much that can be done in adding details, unlike plastic kits. 'Cobra King' was much photographed, so there are plenty of references available for the modeler.

Step 1. One feature that can be added to the turret of the basic model is a .50 calibre anti-aircraft heavy machine gun. Not all Shermans had one, but 'Cobra King' did. There was not much external stowage, apart from a few boxes placed on a plank of wood between the fenders on the front. A strip of plasticard was cut

The basic model M18.

Stowage has been added. The pintle-mounted machine gun is from the spares box.

to size and added to the correct position, then a few boxes and a tarp were added.

Step 2. Prime and paint the model as described previously.

Step 3. When applying the decals, cut as close to the decal as possible, then dip it in cooled boiled water. This reduces the chances of a decal 'silvering', which happens when oxygen is trapped between the surface of the model and decal when dry. The process of boiling the water reduces the amount of oxygen in water and reduces the chances of silvering.

Remove the decal from the water, then apply the decal to the desired location with the aid of a soft brush. A product called Micro Set will help the decal adhere to the surface, while Micro Sol is useful if the decal is to be applied over an uneven surface, as it softens the decal and results in a realistic painted-on look.

One word of warning when using these products, they should be left to dry. Micro Sol will wrinkle the decal when it is wet, but this will disappear once it dries. Repeat this process until the whole model is completed, then leave to dry for twenty-four hours and apply a thin coat of matt varnish.

Step 4. The model is weathered with MIG 1405 'Dark Mud' and P232 'Dry Mud'. Follow the instructions for weathering given for the M4A2 Sherman tank (*see* Chapter 2).

Micro Sol and Micro Set provide a two-part solution when applying water slide decals. They are easy to use and give good results. Make sure that the decals are not touched until they are fully dry.

M18 HELLCAT

The M18 Hellcat, otherwise known as the 76mm Gun Motor Carriage M18, or the M18 GMC, was the fastest American tracked armoured fighting vehicle (AFV) with a road speed of about 80km/h (50mph). Indeed it was the fastest American tracked AFV until 1980, when the M1 Abrams entered service with the US Army.

The M18 was arguably the best American tank destroyer of WWII, with a kill ratio exceeding any other US tank destroyer or tank of its time. Some 2,500 M18s were produced from July 1943 to October 1944 by the Buick division of General Motors.

Armed with a 76mm M1A1 gun and capable of high speed, this lightly armoured and yet very nimble tank destroyer made its mark in many battles in Europe, most notably at the Battle of Arracourt in September 1944. The 704th Tank Destroyer Battalion was attached to the 4th Armored Division as part of Patton's 3rd Army when a German counter-attack was launched by the 5th Panzer Army under the command of General Hasso von Manteuffel. The objective was to recapture the town of Lunéville as part of a counteroffensive against advancing US forces in France as well as the elimination of the US XII Corps bridgehead over the Moselle river.

On 19 September 1944 Lt Edwin Leiper led a platoon of M18s that knocked out five German tanks in only five minutes, with the loss of only one M18. Ten minutes later a further ten German tanks were knocked out, many of which were the feared Panthers of Panzer Brigade 113.

The speed and manoeuvrability of the M18 was a big factor in this success. The Battle of Arracourt continued until 29 September, by when the Germans had lost some 200 tanks and self-propelled guns, and the Americans had lost twenty-five tanks and seven tank destroyers.

The next notable use of the M18 was during the Battle of the Bulge between 16 December 1944 and 25 January 1945, which was the last major German offensive in the West during the war. It was launched through the thick woods of the Ardennes forests and aimed to catch the Allies by surprise.

Many engagements of varying sizes took place during this battle, but the exploits of Team Desobry, a mixed task force of infantry and armour of the 10th Armored Division, are of particular interest. On 19/20 December Team Desobry was assigned to defend the town of Noville, located about 7km (4 miles) north-northeast of Bastogne. With just four M18s this force defended against attacks from 2nd Panzer Division and during that time destroyed some thirty German tanks and inflicted between 500 and 1,000 casualties. The M18s were credited with a large number of the tanks destroyed, which again proved the M18 as an invaluable and versatile vehicle, whose speed and hitting power were put to effective use.

Modelling the M18 Hellcat

This a Milicast resin kit because, at the time of writing, there are no plastic kits on the market in either 1:76 or 1:72 scales. Milicast offers a simple but superbly

The M18 model is constructed. The side skirts that go on the front of the model have been left off at this stage to enable better access for painting the tracks and wheels.

The stowage on the rear has been added from the spares box.

detailed kit, with only a few parts, that builds into a very good M18. A good reference source is recommended. Bear in mind that when it comes to adding the breach, this was rotated 30 degrees. The turret in the Hellcat was small and the gunner needed room, so to aid this the designers rotated the gun breach to give the gunner the room he needed.

Step 1. Lay out all the parts and check them over. This is important as it helps in familiarizing oneself with them as well as identifying any blemishes, which can be common in resin kits. A sharp craft knife is essential, preferably using a new blade for each build, as a blunt blade will not do.

Follow the instructions to build the kit but do not attach the sides of the mudguards at this stage, as this will hinder the painting of the running gear and tracks.

Once the model has been constructed, leave it for twenty-four hours to allow the glue to set and then wash in warm water with mild detergent to remove any grease or dirt. Take care not to knock off the fine details.

Step 2. Even though this model is very detailed, there are one or two things that can be done to enhance it. An antenna can be made by cutting a piece of steel wire to length and fashioning a new holder from Green Stuff. Check the correct shape against a reference source as not all antennas were the same. Leave a little of the antenna showing through the bottom: this can then be placed into the hole provided on the turret roof.

Photos of an M18 will show how the crews tied on items such as extra fuel, rations, personal items wrapped in blankets and tarpaulins. They did this because there was simply no room inside the vehicle for these items. The way this is done is important as they never blocked vision ports, weapons, exhausts or air-intakes. Once the arrangement of the stowage is satisfactory, prime the model for painting.

Step 3. Paint the model following the same procedure as with the M15 (*see* Chapter 4), but with the additional techniques described here.

Once you have applied the basic colours and highlighted and filtered them, leave to dry for twenty-four hours. Then apply a coat of satin varnish to protect the paint, and when dry wash the model with a dark brown enamel wash, and again leave to dry for twenty-four hours. When this is dry, mix some Vallejo 887 'Brown Violet' with a little white added and, using a broad brush, dry brush the whole model. Use a broad flat brush for larger areas and change to a smaller brush for more detailed areas. Dip the tip of the brush lightly in the paint, then wipe off the excess paint with a tissue or cloth. Wipe the brush across the palm of your hand. If the paint only lightly covers the hand and leaves nothing in the creases, then the amount of paint left on the brush is correct. Dry brushing helps to make the model appear more used and rugged, but be careful not to overdo the effect.

When this is dry, apply a coat of satin varnish and leave to dry thoroughly.

Step 4. Apply decals following the guidance in the instructions for the M4A3E2 above.

Once the decals have been applied, leave them to dry for twenty-four hours and finally apply a thin coat of matt varnish.

LEFT: Apply a wash to the joints of the various panels with a fine brush. This helps to make the details 'pop' out and become more pronounced,

BELOW: Apply a dry brush of the original Olive Drab lightened to the upper surfaces. We use Vallejo 124 'Iraqi Sand' mixed 13 with Vallejo 889 'Olive Brown'. A light, dusty effect is all that is needed.

Step 5. Weather the model over a sheet of paper. This will collect any pigment that does not adhere to the model, and so can be collected and reused. With a brush apply some MIG Pigment Fixer to the tracks and running gear. Remember that at the time there were few good roads in Europe and the tank was used during a cold and wet winter, so mud would be prominent. With this in mind, and after checking photos of the actual vehicle, apply some MIG 1405 'Dark Mud' pigment to the tracks and running gear.

Leave this to dry for a few minutes and then apply fixer to certain upper areas, such as around the hatches, tools and stowage, then apply some 'Dry Mud' pigment sparingly to these areas as well as a little to the running gear.

When the pigments have been left to dry overnight, take a broad brush and go over the whole model lightly. This removes any excess pigment as well as blending it all together for a more realistic and pleasing effect.

LEFT: The intended effect should be subtle, yet effective, and not overpowering.

BELOW: The completed M18 with crew.

THE WILLYS ARMOURED JEEP

No book on modelling the US Army of WWII would be complete without mention of what must be the most iconic vehicle of the war. The Willys Jeep was a real workhorse and jack of all trades. The Willys Jeep has done everything from scouting and communications to anti-tank and personnel carrying. This rugged little 4 × 4 was and remains a true icon of military vehicles of the twentieth century: by 1968 some one million had been built in America alone.

The example used is the armoured reconnaissance version, which was mainly produced by field workshops to a typical design. The front and sides were armoured, with the addition of 1in plate steel to the windshield, which replaced the front of the radiator grille, and to the side area, which provided protection from small arms fire. This was actually just one sheet of steel, cut to shape with two vision slots added and folded in three. These Jeeps were used mainly from September 1944 by various units until the end of the war, and they can be seen in a variety of styles. This version is based on a Jeep used by the 82nd Airborne Division during Operation *Market Garden*.

Modelling the Willys armoured Jeep

This model is based around an Airfix kit with the armour made from plasticard. When starting to build the kit, choose the American version and not the Airborne Jeep, as this was only used by the British.

Step 1. Construct the kit following the instructions. When it comes to adding the sides of the jeep body, assembly will be easier if the rear is also attached at this point. The windscreen is not required as this was removed so that the new armour could be fitted with ease. Also leave off the wing mirror (Part B23), as this is not needed.

A Jeep used for reconnaisance would be fitted with a pintle-mounted .30 calibre machine gun. Leave the assembled model aside so that the glue may properly cure before moving on to making and fitting the armour.

Step 2. The tools needed are a sharp craft knife, a steel ruler, a pen or pencil and 10 thou plasticard.

Start by marking out the armour, which should be 45mm long by 9mm high, and then divide this by

Airfix makes a truly superb kit that contains the options to build either an American or British Jeep. It also has a trailer and a M1A1 75mm Pack Howitzer.

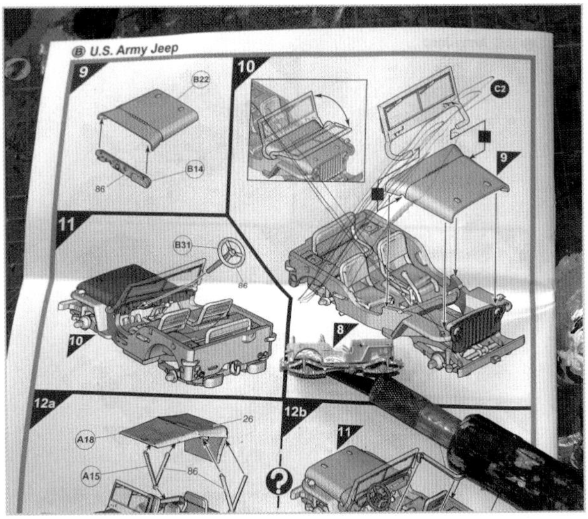

ABOVE: Follow the instructions to build the basic model.

LEFT: The basic model is constructed.

three lengthways. Mark the driver's vision slit (this should be 5mm long by 1.5mm high) and the notch to allow a clear field of fire for the machine-gun mounted on the rear. These armoured Jeeps varied as some were field modifications of existing Jeeps, so a little variation in modelling one is fine.

Step 3. Cut the armour out as one strip, and then cut into three pieces. Two of these will form the sides and the other will form the front of the armour where the windscreen would have been. Attach this piece where the bonnet hinges to the jeep, just where the windscreen would have sat when upright. Now make the two corner pieces from plasticard. These should be angled and shaped so that they fit snugly into the curve of the bucket (the correct name for a Willys Jeep body).

Cut a strip of white paper and place it behind the armoured side plate so that it meets against the front piece. Using a pencil, trace the shape of the space between the two.

Draw in the shape with a pencil so that it is more pronounced. When the shape is satisfactory, cut it out. This will provide a template that will work for both sides.

Now draw around the paper template placed on the plasticard and cut out both sides with a very sharp pair of scissors. Carefully dry fit the two pieces and

LEFT: Clearly mark out the pieces needed to make the armour.

BELOW: The three pieces are placed like this, then fixed in place.

ABOVE LEFT: This part of the build needs care.

ABOVE RIGHT: One of the pieces for the side armour.

LEFT: The two pieces are now added carefully.

ABOVE: The assembled armoured Jeep complete with an armoured plate to cover the radiator. This is cut to size to fit the model, leaving the headlights showing, and results in a simple yet effective model.

GLUES TO USE WITH HARD PLASTIC KITS

There are several brands of liquid polystyrene cement that are supplied in glass bottles and need to be applied with a brush. This type of cement is great when working with plasticard, since it dries quickly as well as being accurate to use.

trim them to get an exact fit. The templates were deliberately oversized when they were copied onto the plasticard to allow room for such trimming and fitting. When the fit is correct, glue into position using liquid cement, as this is the best type of glue when working with plasticard.

Step 4. Now cut out a piece of plasticard 9 × 8mm to go in front of the radiator, as all armoured Jeeps had this. Leave enough room for the headlights to be seen. Finally, fill in the holes that were not needed as the windscreen and wing mirror has not been fitted.

Step 5. To paint the Jeep simply follow the instructions for the Pershing in Chapter 7. Once this is finished, base the model as this will help to protect the wheels.

PAINTING GENERAL GEORGE S. PATTON

This book would not be complete without one of the most important military figures of WWII: George S. Patton jnr. As most of the models covered in this chapter, and indeed the next, are from units of his 3rd Army, it is very apt that a description is given here of how to paint a figure to represent him.

This 28mm tall metal miniature has been sculpted wearing his customary 'Ike Jacket' and riding breeches, which were very appropriate as Patton was a cavalry man.

Step 1. Apply a thin priming coat of matt black paint. This picks out the details on the figure and will help to reveal the detail to be painted.

Step 2. Paint the flesh areas, first using as a base colour AK3073 'Red Brown Leather'. Then lighten the base colour by adding Vallejo 955 'Flat Flesh' and use this for highlighting. Keep lightening the paint and highlighting the raised area until the desired effect is achieved. The riding boots, belt and pistol holster should also be base coated with 'Red Brown Leather' at this time.

Step 3. Base coat the jacket with AK3074 'Brown Olive Drab'. The breeches are base coated with AK3075 'US Field Drab' and the helmet with Vallejo 887 'Brown Violet'.

Step 4. Start to highlight the jacket and breeches, adding a little white to the respective colours used and going over the raised areas of the uniform. The helmet is also highlighted using 'Brown Violet' with just a little white added. Always take care not to add too much white, since adding only a little amount at a time will help to achieve a subtle effect. Also apply a wash of Vallejo 73.200 'Sepia Shade' to the leather of the boots and belt/holster to give added depth.

Step 5. Now add details. At the time under consideration Patton was a Lieutenant General – a three-star general. Paint three stars on each shoulder as well as three stars on his helmet. The belt buckle is painted gold. The ribbons are painted various colours, in this case red, blue, yellow and white. The riding crop was painted with Vallejo 311 'New Wood' and the leather part of the riding crop is painted Vallejo 984 'Flat Brown'. When the figure is dry, apply a coat of varnish and base.

The 28mm figure that will become General George S. Patton.

The flesh areas and riding boots, belt and pistol holder are all base coated.

The jacket, breeches and helmet are base coated.

Highlighting is added to the jacket, breeches and helmet.

Apply a wash of 'Sepia Shade' to the leather of the boots and the belt/holster.

The details have been added and the model is finished with a coat of varnish.

7 The End of the War in Europe, March–May 1945

THIS CHAPTER WILL COVER some of the vehicles used in the months leading up to VE Day on 8 May 1945. The uniforms worn by the GIs were the same as those worn in the Ardennes (*see* Chapter 7). Although only a few M26 Pershing Heavy Tanks were used in combat, the important role they played in the assault on the Ludendorff railway bridge at Remagen in March 1945, when ten Pershings attached to the 2nd Armored Division help secure the last intact bridge over the River Rhine leading into Germany, justifies their inclusion. They were also involved in the battle for Cologne that same month.

Even though only a few months remained until the eventual surrender, the German armies still fought with their usual skill and tenacity in defence of their homeland. The Allied armies faced some of their toughest battles during those final months and experienced some of the highest casualty rates since landing in Normandy in June 1944.

During the last months of WWII the US Army started to receive new vehicles, such as the M26 Pershing. This had been designed in 1942 but production did not start until November 1944, when it was finally decided that there was a real need for a heavier tank armed with an 80mm gun. Previously it had been thought that up-gunning the M4 Sherman with a 76mm gun would be adequate, but when facing the heavier Germans tanks, such as the Tiger and Panther, it was clear that the Sherman was no match for them. It has to be remembered that the

'To the victor the spoils': GIs relaxing, Germany, May 1945.

ABOVE: T26 Pershing, Cologne, 1945.

BELOW: M36 Jackson Tank Destroyer, Germany, spring 1945.

M4 Sherman was designed to combat German tanks such as the Panzer III, which was the main German battle tank up to 1943. However, by 1944 the Panzer IV was being used in very large numbers and, while the Sherman could cope with it, its gun was no match for the 7.5cm KWK 40 gun with which the Panzer IV was equipped from 1942. The M4 was up-gunned to the 76mm, but this gun was still no match for the Panther or Tiger. Production of the M26 Pershing finally started in November 1944 and ten were built that month at the Fisher Tank Arsenal. This was increased to thirty in December, seventy in January and 132 in February 1945. This rate of production continued on throughout 1945 and in total more than 2,000 were produced.

On 22 December 1944 a shipment of twenty vehicles, then designated T26E3, was ordered to be deployed to Europe. These arrived on 20 January 1945 and were the only T26s to see combat. It may seem strange to choose to model a tank that was used in such limited numbers, but there are two good reasons for this: first, because the T26 had been anticipated and wanted by US tank crews for such a long time; and second, the T26 saw action at Remagen and Cologne in two of the best-known skirmishes of the closing months of the war in Europe. It was at Cologne that a T26 belonging to the 3rd Armored Division engaged and destroyed a Panther during one of the most famous tank duels of the war.

The M36 Jackson was the last of the American Tank Destroyers developed during WWII. It was designed in 1943, first saw action in October 1944 and was still in use with the US Army during the Korean War. Some re-engined examples were still serving in the 1990s during the Yugoslavian civil war. The M36 mounted a 90mm M3 gun that was designed to take on and destroy the heavier German tanks such as the Tiger and Panther. American Tank Destroyer doctrine was to mount a large-calibre anti-tank gun on a lightly armoured vehicle, for example the M18, so that it could engage enemy tanks but move out of trouble using its advantage of speed. This was believed to negate the need for heavier tanks and was the main reason the M26 did not start production until November 1944. Nevertheless, the US military produced some fine vehicles, including the M36 Jackson, that performed their role well and accounted for large numbers of German tanks. These last few months of the war in Europe saw the swansong of the American tank destroyer and the advent of the heavy tank, which has continued to evolve into the modern American main battle tanks such as the M1 Abrams.

An M4A3E8 Sherman and M5 Stuart support the infantry as they move up during the advance into Germany, early 1945.

MODELLING THE T26 PERSHING HEAVY TANK

The 1:72 scale model by the Chinese firm Trumpeter is a superb kit that requires little work. It includes decals for the T26 mentioned earlier, belonging to the 3rd Armored Division and commanded by Sergeant Robert Early, which took part in a famous duel against a Panther at Cologne in March 1945. The only additional part needed is a new brass barrel obtained from the Polish company RB Model. The track units supplied with this kit are very good but can cause problems for the novice. They are 'link and length' tracks and need to be assembled and attached to the model. With larger-scale models these are assembled then placed on the running gear, but with this model it is better to assemble them directly onto the running gear as it makes for a stronger completed item.

Step 1. First take a look at the parts and plans, and put aside those that are not needed immediately. Select the required track and running gear parts and assemble following the instructions supplied with the kit.

When building the running gear it is a good idea to first check how many wheels and other components are needed. As the construction of each set is completed, place the completed sections away from the work area but separately from each other. When the running gear is assembled, make sure all the wheels are straight and that none is

RIGHT: The Trumpeter kit of a T26 Pershing; the new metal barrel is by RB Model.

BELOW: Assembling the required wheels and running gear this way makes sure the numbers are correct and nothing has been misplaced.

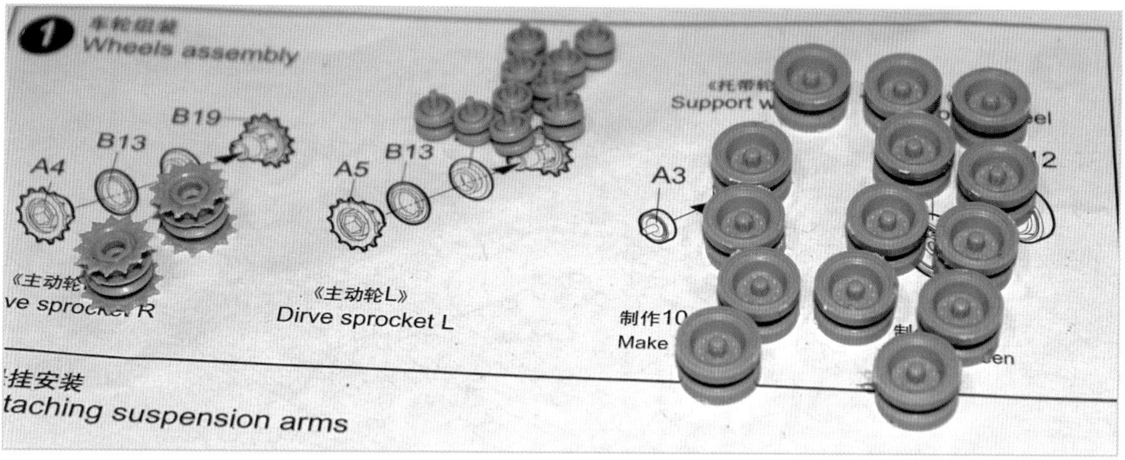

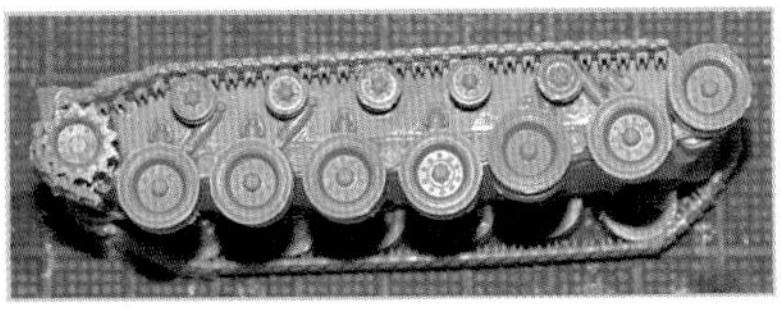

ABOVE: Link and length tracks take longer to fit than either vinyl or rubber tracks, but the finished result always looks more realistic.

RIGHT: The constructed kit, minus the main gun.

crooked or bent. Leave the whole assembly to one side for twenty-four hours to allow the glue to fully cure. There are many small parts in this construction, so it is best to have patience and wait until the glue cures properly and the assembly is solid enough to work with.

Step 2. The next step is to assemble the tracks. This will take time but the result looks realistic. Liquid cement is the best glue for this job. Start on the drive sprockets by assembling the tracks there, and then add the long pieces of track that run along the idler wheels at the top. Pay careful attention to the number and type of track pieces that are required to go around each drive sprocket. This is very important as this stage will dictate how everything else looks when the model is finished. If an error is made here, the whole track assembly will look uneven. Once the longer upper track piece is correctly in place, add the track pieces to the rear idler wheel, working around this wheel until all the required pieces are used.

Now fit the long lower piece of track: if this fails to meet properly, as it does with the track added to the drive sprocket, check the work as some adjustment may be required, or simply add another piece of track, which should bridge the gap. If the gap is too wide, again recheck the work and make sure that all the parts have been correctly positioned. This process is repeated until both sides are complete. The track should look realistic and level on both the idler wheel and drive sprocket. Then brush some liquid cement over the track, taking care not to use too much. This will ensure there are no dry joints and will secure the pieces in place. Then leave to dry for a few hours.

Step 3. Now build the rest of the kit following the instructions provided. Do not fit the heavy machine gun mounted on the turret roof, as the Pershing at Cologne did not have it and this model will be true to that vehicle. Before fitting the main gun, check for any gaps that may be present between the joins of the two halves of the turret. Any minor gaps can be quickly filled with modelling putty. Because the main gun has not been fitted, there will be more room for filling and sanding. When that is done, fit the barrel. The antennas can then be made from thin wire. Next add stowage, making sure that the turret can still rotate 360 degrees, as stowage should not prevent this.

Step 4. Prime the model and leave to dry for a few hours before airbrushing. Then start by thinning the paint so it can be used in the airbrush. The paint is 'Olive Drab' manufactured by the Japanese firm Mr Hobby. This should be thinned with acrylic thinners at a ratio of 50:50. If the paint is too thick, it will not flow through the airbrush freely and the results will be poor. Mix the thinner and paint together thoroughly: place in a jam jar with a lid and shake for two minutes. Then pour the thinned paint into the side cup of the airbrush, taking care not to overfill the cup, filling it halfway so it can be topped up as needed.

When starting to paint the model, do not try to cover the whole model in one coat. It is best to apply thin coats so that they dry quickly and can be

The model is now ready to be primed.

The basic coat has now been applied to the T26 using an airbrush.

recoated. It may take two or three coats to get a good finish. Start by painting the recessed areas, then the bottom, sides and top. The turret is always painted separately. Taking plenty of time at this stage will repay the effort. Once a satisfactory result has been achieved, leave it aside to dry for twenty-four hours. Even though this is acrylic paint, it still needs time to dry properly.

Step 5. Now add a few highlights by lightening the original colour with just a little white, and then adding thinner at a ratio of 60 parts thinner to 40 parts paint. Mix by shaking in a jar. Then add this to the cup of the airbrush. Test the paint flow and adjust until it gives a fine line. In the case of the Aztek airbrush, just use the red nozzle. This is the tricky part. Recessed areas should be avoided, so carefully apply a thin layer of paint to the sides of the turret and turret roof, as well as the upper parts of the fenders. This desired effect is to create a feeling of shade, so only paint areas that will catch the light. If done well the difference will not be too obvious as this aspect of painting should not stand out. When allowed to dry for a couple of hours, a subtle gradation from a mild light to a dark effect should be visible.

The airbrush is used to highlight the model before moving on.

Step 6. A pin wash is a dark wash that is applied to the recesses as well as the panel lines. This gives an extra illusion of depth to the model. You should now see the highlights starting to stand out. Allow ten minutes for the pin wash to settle and then apply the filter over the entire model using a good quality medium-sized brush. Do not use too much filter, however, as the model should not be flooded. Applying the filter now, and using a good quality brush, will achieve a very natural effect as it will blend into the pin wash, leaving a perfect light to dark effect.

Step 7. The Vallejo wash for green vehicles filter used here dries to a satin finish, so there is no need to apply a gloss coat to the model. Apply any decals required, then paint the tracks and stowage. Keep the colours used for painting the stowage muted because they need to look a natural part of the model and as such should not overpower the overall look.

Step 8. Apply a light coat of matt varnish to protect the model as well as sealing in the decals, then leave until dry. Some modellers like to 'chip' their model so that it more accurately represents a vehicle that has seen a fair amount of use, but this is not strictly necessary as the T26 was a new vehicle that had only recently arrived in Europe. A lighter 'used' effect can be achieved by applying a little gunmetal to the odd edge here and there. This should not be more than a mere hint, so take care not to overdo this.

For weathering, follow the procedure as outlined for the M4A2 Sherman (*see* Chapter 2), using MIG 1405 'Dark Mud' and P232 'Dry Mud'.

The filter should only be applied to the recessed areas and nowhere else.

A dark green filter will balance the colours used to highlight the base colour.

The stowage has now been painted.

When applying decals, use a soft pointed brush as this will help to position them correctly.

The completed model, now with a commander.

MODELLING THE M36 JACKSON TANK DESTROYER

If the model is to be used for wargaming it is best to use a plastic kit that will result in a strong and robust model. As most model kits are not really designed for use in wargames, the best choice is one made by Armourfast, which manufactures and sells a range of plastic armour kits designed with the wargamer in mind. They are quick to build but are very basic. As such, they need some customization or modification to bring them up to an acceptable standard.

S&S Models makes a range of aftermarket items designed to customize basic kits and make them look more professional. This model has no interior detail within the turret other than the breach, but it is not difficult to add a crew serving the gun.

Inside the box there are enough parts to build two basic M36 Jacksons. Also seen here are the S&S parts that will be needed later.

Step 1. Start by assembling the kit, which is very straightforward to do. This provides a blank canvas, so to speak, on which more detail can be added. Drilling out a small portion of the barrel, using a pin vice and a 1mm drill bit, helps add some more realism.

The S&S aftermarket set is designed for the Armourfast M10 Tank Destroyer, but as both models have the same hull and only the turrets differ, most of the accessories can be used on the M36. In this case, stowage is being added to make the model look more realistic: photos from the time show these vehicles covered in stowage and looking like mobile homes, with even bicycles strapped on. These vehicles looked very lived in, which in fact they were, with everything their crews needed to carry out repairs or for cooking and sleeping being within reach.

Step 2. Before painting, clean off any excess glue that mars the paint finish. An AB Miniatures tank destroyer crew can now be added. A grey primer is next applied to provide a neutral base over which the later colours will be painted. The basic overall colour is 'olive drab', following the procedure laid down for painting tanks in Chapter 6.

ABOVE: Drill out the barrel to a depth of no more than a few millimetres. This is all that is necessary to create the illusion of a hollow barrel.

LEFT: The constructed kit is good, but basic, and this can be improved.

The completed M36, complete with a turret crew. The extra pieces added to the model improve its overall appearance.

THE GI IN GERMANY, 1945

The 1:32 scale Airfix multi-pose kit will build an American GI as he would have looked during the advance into Germany in 1945. The uniform worn at this time was warmer and more suited to the winter conditions: the M-1943 Olive Drab jacket, woollen M-1937 trousers and gloves. Herringbone Twill (HBT) trousers were also worn, but the M-1937 trousers were more popular as they were warmer.

The boots were now the M-1943 combat boots, first introduced in November 1943 but only reaching the front-line units in late 1944. They provided better ankle support than the previous 'roughout' ankle boot and gaiters and kept out the dirt and weather. This is now the GI that most people are familiar with from war films made from the 1950s to the 1970s.

Several options are available with this set, but the configuration chosen here is for a lieutenant armed with a M1 Carbine. This weapon was widely used by junior officers and was in use throughout WWII, even though it was not a hard-hitting weapon by any means.

Step 1. The assembly is the same as for the American infantryman on Okinawa (*see* Chapter 2), but for this officer it is necessary to add a few extra parts that come supplied with the set. Unfortunately they are not covered in the instructions and so this is where good references are required. In this case Windrow and Hawkins's *The World War II GI: US Army Uniforms, 1941–45, in Color Photographs* was invaluable.

Step 2. To arm the figure, a pistol will be added on the right waist, behind the ammunition pouches, with a bayonet situated next to it. As this figure is of an infantry officer, a backpack will also be added. These officers had to live under the same conditions as their men and so carried the same equipment, apart from a few extra items, such as binoculars and a pistol. At this late stage in the war, officers tended to carry the same weapon as their men and did not wear rank insignia, so that they were a less obvious target for enemy snipers. The M1 carbine was carried by both officers and NCOs, so is a good choice here.

Step 3. This kit does not provide rifle slings or straps from which his binoculars can hang, but these are easily made from paper cut into 1mm strips and attached with superglue. These simple and quick techniques help to add extra detail to any figure.

Step 4. Now prime the figure using grey primer: this colour is best for use on larger figures as it helps to

The basic GI model with additions.

After a coat of grey primer, the figure is ready for painting.

The main colours have been added and a start made on the flesh tones.

This shows where the colours should be added to form the base for the next step.

The wooden parts and the boots have been highlighted with dark brown and washed with black ink.

provide a neutral base on which other colours will look their best once dry.

Step 5. Now paint the jacket using AK3071 'Dark Olive Green/M-43 Uniform Green Olive' as the base colour and the trousers with AK3075 'US Field Drab'. Apply washes of thinned ink – black over the jacket and brown over the trousers – to provide the illusion of depth. Next, paint in the face and hands with Vallejo 955 'Flat Flesh', and when dry wash with flesh wash, which again will provide depth for the later colours.

Step 6. Paint the boots and bayonet dark grey.

Step 7. Now using the original colours, but with the addition of a little Vallejo 819 'Iraqi Sand', highlight both the jacket and trousers. Then use Vallejo 924 'Russian Uniform' to base coat the backpack, webbing and water bottle. Highlight them with Vallejo 821 'German Camouflage Beige'. Remember, it is even more important to keep the colours subtle since on large figures, such as these, how you lighten any colour is of paramount importance, and this will help achieve a more pleasing and realistic finish. With this in mind, take plenty of time and work slowly to achieve the desired result.

The rear view of the figure after the details have been highlighted.

Step 8. Paint the rifle sling, pistol holster and the binoculars strap with AK3073 'Red Brown Leather'. Use this colour also to paint the wooden parts of the rifle and spade handle as it will make a good base colour for the next stage.

Step 9. Lighten the original colour with a little white and use this to highlight the helmet. Then move on to the wooden parts of the figure, painting the rifle and spade handle with Vallejo 311 'New Wood', and then highlight these with a little white added. Go around the webbing and backpack with 'German Camouflage Beige'. Add a little white and go over them again for an added layer of highlights. Then paint the buttons, the metal parts of the rifle and bayonet scabbard with gunmetal.

Step 10. It is now necessary to paint the rank insignia on the helmet. The US Army used a horizontal white bar on the rear of a helmet to denote an NCO (non-commissioned officer) and a vertical bar for an officer, which enabled them to be recognized from the rear. Rank insignia made of silvered metal were worn on collars, but these tended to catch the light and attract snipers' attention. Officers often decided to cover them up or not wear them at all on the front line.

This made the helmet markings all the more significant. As this is a figure of an officer, a vertical white bar will be added. This is first done with some light grey paint and then going over it with white paint. On the front paint a single small lieutenant bar.

Step 11. All that remains is to apply a wash of thinned-down dark brown over the figure, except for the hands and face. This helps to tie in all the other colours for a more effective look. Following these simple steps will give a figure that accurately represents an officer on the front line of the advance into Germany in early 1945.

LEFT: The buttons have all been painted as well as the officer's bar on the rear of his helmet.

BELOW: The completed figure.

M8 ARMOURED CAR 'GREYHOUND'

The M8 armoured car, otherwise known as the 'Greyhound', served in cavalry reconnaissance units and filled the gap between the M3 and M5 Stuart, as well as the M3 scout car. The M8 was a six-wheeled scout car armed with a 37mm M6 gun for which it carried some eighty rounds of ammunition. A coaxial .30 calibre Browning was also fitted. When it was found that the M8 needed an anti-aircraft machine gun, a .50 calibre M2 was retro-fitted on a ring mount to the turret on all existing models. The M8 served with the US and British armies, and with the Free French.

The M8 was a fast and rugged vehicle that fulfilled its role perfectly. While not heavily armoured, it could take on lighter German armoured cars. However, it was not a match for the later German Puma armoured car, which mounted a 50mm gun that could easily penetrate the M8's thin armour (it could could even be penetrated by 20mm guns). Despite this drawback, the speed and agility of this armoured car made it a dangerous adversary during engagements with other reconnaissance vehicles. The crews added sandbags to the floors of their vehicles to help boost the protection offered by the thinner armour on the floor that could easily be penetrated by mines. Reconnaissance units equipped with M8s were the 'eyes and ears' of an advance, always in the front and generally the first to encounter enemy units. During withdrawals they would help form a protective screen for other units.

Modelling the M8 Greyhound

There are not many M8 armoured car kits available at the time of writing: Italeri used to produce one, but this is now hard to find. This is a resin version produced by Hobby Den, which is a simple but serviceable model of an M8 Greyhound.

Step 1. Start by putting the model together. Fortunately this model has only a few parts. Wash the kit with warm soapy water to remove any release agent left over from the moulding process.

Step 2. It is now necessary to add an anti-aircraft machine gun and some stowage. It was common for

The basic model of the M8.

The added stowage is seen here with the .50 calibre anti-aircraft machine gun.

The primed model is now ready to paint.

M8 crews to add plenty of stowage of all types to their vehicles, as they could be out on patrol for a long time and needed to be as self-sufficient as possible.

Step 3. Prime the model in black. Then paint it with olive drab, applying several even coats and allowing them to dry between coats. Now lightly brush over the entire model with the base colour with a little white added, paying attention to the raised areas.

Next apply an enamel pin wash to the panel lines and recesses of the model with a fine brush. This will make the details stand out, adding depth to the model.

Step 4. Once the pin wash has dried, paint the stowage in appropriate colours, such as khaki, light brown and olive green. Then wash over the vehicle with a very transparent, diluted version of the pin wash to tie together the whole paint effect of the stowage and model for a realistic effect. This is a slightly different technique to those already described, but when done with care it does create a pleasing effect.

Step 5. Finally apply the decals and then weather the model using the steps outlined in Chapter 2.

The base colour of Olive Drab has been applied.

Brushing over a lightened version of Olive Drab helps to pick out hidden detail.

ABOVE LEFT: The detail on the model is now a little too prominent. Pin wash will help to blend the colours together.

ABOVE RIGHT: The M8 with all the stowage painted. The next step is to apply a wash.

LEFT: The difference that a wash can make is obvious after it has dried.

BELOW: Two finished M8s.

8 Working with Soft Plastic Soldiers and Basing Figures

SO FAR THIS BOOK has covered metal and hard polystyrene (PS) figures, which are currently the two most common materials from which wargames figures are made. Metal is fairly straightforward to work with and because it does not require the large industrial machinery needed to produce hard polystyrene figures, it is often the preferred material for smaller companies, especially wargaming manufacturers. Hard polystyrene is used in the production of kits, such as those manufactured by Airfix. It is fairly easy to work with and gives greater scope for conversion work when desired. PS figures are also light, which makes the task of transporting them much easier than their metal counterparts.

Soft plastic soldiers are made from a type of polyethylene (PE) or polypropylene (PP) and are mass produced. They are softer and bend easily, which is a feature of the material from which they are made. There are pros and cons to wargaming with these figures. They are inexpensive compared to even their hard polystyrene cousins (working out at about one-fifth of the price) and as such are perfect for the newcomer to the hobby who has limited means. They are also easily converted and the poses can be altered slightly, which makes them more versatile than metal figures. However, one of the drawbacks is that the PE or PP does not take paint very well, in fact, paint can and will peel off unless you are first prepared to undertake a fair amount of work. Nonetheless these figures, which have been around since the 1970s, are readily available in most model and toy shops and are still a large part of the hobby today.

I started WWII wargaming with a set of Esci plastic American infantry in 1984, and I still have them, although they no longer get used. They are still in very good condition and the paint is fully intact after all these years, because even then I prepared them properly.

The variety of ranges available is now vast, with even more choice than when I started. There are sets for nearly every nation that fought during WWII so the wargamer is faced with an almost endless variety and choice. These are available from companies such as Airfix, Italeri, Caesar and Orion. Some have now switched to a less pliable plastic that aids with the adhesion of paint, but good preparation is still required so that long-lasting results are achieved.

When you purchase a box of figures, you will see that they are attached to runners. It is best to leave these on as they help in the first stages of preparation. For this example I have chosen a set of American tank riders made by HaT, one of the many companies that now produce figures in plastic.

One other reason for keeping the figures on their frame is that it will make the process of painting them

US Army figures by HaT Toys.

LEFT: After washing allow the figures to dry.

BELOW: Several brands of plastic primer are available.

much easier. As they are tank riders they do not have a base, so painting them while still on the frame makes sense. This way the frame can be held and not the figure, making for a better finish.

Step 1. Using washing up liquid added to warm, not hot, water, wash the figures and then allow to dry.

Step 2. Painting these plastic figures is really not that different from painting any other wargame figure made from either metal or hard plastic, but a little more preparation is needed to achieve good results. When painting these figures, preparation is the key. Proper preparation now will pay dividends later when painting.

Several techniques can be used to prevent the paint from coming off, but the most reliable is using a light coat of plastic primer. This is available from car accessory retailers and it comes as either a clear lacquer or as a grey paint, both of which will work perfectly well. Once the primer is dry, apply a second light coat and leave this to dry for a couple of hours. If clear lacquer has been used and a neutral base is preferred, a coat of standard primer can be applied once the lacquer is dry.

Step 3. Now paint the figure as normal, and the hard work put in will stay where it should and not peel. These models are going to depict GIs taking part in the Normandy breakout at the end of July 1944. Details of the colours to use and the procedure for painting infantry for this campaign will be found in Chapter 5. Once painted, apply a coat of gloss varnish.

This picture shows the figures we are painting still attached to the mounting frame, which helps when painting plastic vehicle crew figures. When painted, carefully remove the required figures with a sharp knife.

When this is dry apply two coats of matt varnish. After allowing time to dry, remove the chosen figures from the frame using a scalpel fitted with a new blade. Any unpainted areas that were attached to the frame can then be touched in with the appropriate colour.

Preparing a plastic figure in this way is not as difficult as it first appears. The results can be very pleasing as well as long lasting.

A few tricks can be used when it comes to changing poses. Very hot, not boiling, water has been used for decades by both modellers and wargamers to help get the desired pose. Although this method has its limitations, it can also be used to cure any weapons that have been 'bent'. The trick when using this method is to dip the re-posed figure into cold water straightaway, as this then fixes the new pose.

BASING FIGURES

The subject of basing figures and models has been mentioned during the course of the previous chapters, but what is a base, and what is its purpose? A base has many functions, the main one being to provide stability to a figure. Wargames figures come with a small cast-on base and need something larger to enable them to stand freely without falling over at the slightest tremor. Bases can also provide protection to both figures and models. This is especially true for vehicles with wheels, which can be very vulnerable to damage during use. A well-presented base will enhance the look of a figure or model and help bring it to life. Basing is a simple and effective way of finishing a figure or model.

It is recommended that all wheeled vehicles should be based, but tanks or half-tracks can be based according to preference. If a tank or half-track features as part of a diorama or towing something such as a gun, it would need to be based, as a base will provide both durability and support. The requirements for basing any figure or model are dried builder's sand, which is a cheap material available from any builder's merchant or DIY shop, and PVA glue. The acrylic paint used to paint bases can be bought from art suppliers. The rough texture of the sand will ruin more expensive brushes, so using a less expensive alternative is best.

The M2 Half-track (*see* Chapter 4) has been chosen as an example of how to base a model, but this time it will be towing a 57mm anti-tank gun.

Step 1. Cut out the base from 40 thou plasticard and then glue the half-track in position, followed by the gun. Add some reinforcing strips of the same plasticard to strengthen the area under the gun. An alternative way would be to use a thicker base, but experience has shown that this type of plastic is fine for basing models like this.

Step 2. Next paint the base in an appropriate colour. In this example light brown has been chosen to represent a dry country. Leave to dry.

Step 3. When the paint is completely dry, take a dark sand colour that is lighter than the base colour and lightly brush this over the original paint, while still leaving some of this to show through. Add a little white paint to the sand colour and highlight the base by brushing this over it very lightly. This should give a pleasant 3D effect.

Step 4. Applying the same pigments that were used to weather the model, in this case starting with MIG P038 'Africa Earth' and then P030 'Beach Sand', blend both pigments in as this M2 Half-track is shown in the Sicilian summer and needs to look dusty. There should also be some grass, so a few tufts of greenery and dried scrub will look the part.

READY-MADE BASES

Commercially available, ready-made bases come in several shapes and sizes, as well as in materials such as plastic and MDF. They can be used to mount figures as well as guns and vehicles.

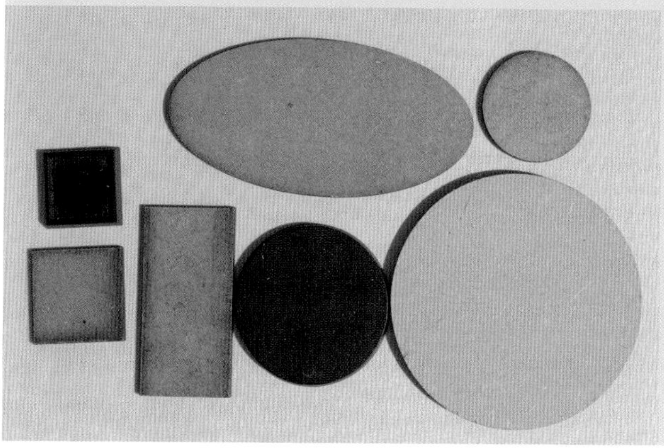

LEFT: A selection of commercially available bases.

ABOVE: A completed base.

LEFT: The two models are now in position on the base and the reinforcing strips can clearly be seen.

BELOW: Paint the base and then leave it to dry thoroughly, preferably overnight.

TOP: Brushing over the first colour will provide the base colours for the pigments. This needs to be done in a subtle way so the effect is gradual.

ABOVE: When using weathering pigments, always start from dark to light, and work them in well with a rough brush that will remove excess pigments effectively without damaging the paintwork of the model.

LEFT: Tufts come in many colours as well as height. They are really useful when working on bases of any size.

Useful Contacts

AB Figures
Eureka Miniatures, 148 Poath Road,
3166 Hughesdale, VIC, Australia
www.abfigures.com

Available in the UK from
Fighting 15s, Green Butts, Colwell Road,
Freshwater, Isle of Wight PO40 9SL
www.fighting15sshop.co.uk

Acrylicos Vallejo SL
AP 337, 08800 Vilanova i la Geltrú,
Barcelona, Spain
www.acrylicosvallejo.com

AMMO of Mig Jimenez SL
Avenida Villatuerta 31, 31132 Villatuerta,
Navarra, Spain
www.migjimenez.com

Armourfast
Unit 4, Orsett Industrial Park,
Stanford Road,
Orsett, Grays, Essex RM16 3BX
www.armourfast.com

CP Models and TQD Castings
Mark Dixon, 7 Tennyson Road, Hinckley,
Leicestershire LE10 0TH
https://cpmodels.co.uk

Dremel Europe
www.dremeleurope.com

Elhiem Figures
65 St Kenelms Road, Romsley,
Worcestershire B62 0PG
www.elhiem.co.uk

The Hobby Den
Unit F3, Enterprise Centre,
Melitta Road, Kildare Town,
Co. Kildare, Ireland
www.thehobbyden.com

Milicast Models
9 Rannoch Street, Battlefield,
Glasgow G44 4DF
www.milicast.com

Raventhorpe Miniatures
2 Bygot Lane, Cherry Burton.
Beverley, North Humberside
HU17 7RN

S&S Models
22 Briar Close, Burnham-on-Sea,
Somerset TA8 1HU
www.sandsmodels.com

Bibliography

THE FOLLOWING BOOKS HAVE been useful while working on this book and are listed for the reader who wishes to learn more about the various themes covered here.

Charbonnier, P., *Allied Soldiers of World War Two* (Histoire & Collections, 1993)

Deschodt, C., and L. Rouger, *D-Day Paratroopers: The Americans* (Histoire & Collections, 2011)

Gander, T., *US Halftracks: M2, M3, M5, M9, Military Vehicles in Detail 3* (Ian Allan, 2004)

Restayn, J., *Tanks of World War Two* (Histoire & Collections, 1998)

Windrow, R., and T. Hawkins, *The World War II GI: US Army Uniforms, 1941–45, in Color Photographs* (1993) (The Crowood Press, 2008)

Index

Abrams M1 Tank 104
Airborne Division, 82nd ('All American') 59, 69, 77–80, 88, 97
101st ('Screaming Eagles') 69, 77–80,8, 89
airbrushes 15–16
ammunition belts 26
Anderson, Gen. Kenneth 42
antenna, making 94
anti-aircraft half-track 59–63
Ardennes 93 *see also* Bulge, Battle of the
Arlington National Cemetery 20
armband *see* brassard 43
armoured car, Greyhound 114–17
Arnhem 88
Arracourt, Battle of 93
atom bombs 39
Autocar Company 46, 64

Bangalore Torpedo 74, 76
bases & basing 16–17, 120–2
Bastogne 88
Bataan 18
bayonets 73
Betio 26, 27, 30
bocage, problems of 71–2
boots design 88, 112
Bradley, Gen. Omar 46, 72
brassard (armband) 43, 44
Browning anti-aircraft gun 25–6
Browning automatic Rifle (BAR) 43
Browning M1917 25–6
Bulge, Battle of the 88, 93

Caen 70
camouflage, painting 29
camouflage patterns 18, 26, 27
Carrickfergus 59
chipping 34, 36
clamps 12–13
Cologne 102, 104, 105
combat engineers 77
Creighton Abrams 81
Culin Prong 71, 72, 83–4
Culin, Sgt Curtis G. 72
Cunningham, Admiral Andrew 42
Cunningham, Cdr Winfield S. 19
cutting mat 12
cyanoacrylate (superglue) 13, 57, 59, 88

Darby, Col William Orlando 59
D-Day 69–84
decals, applying 33, 48, 62–3, 92
Desobry, Team 93
Devereux, Maj. James P.S. 19
Diamond T Company 46, 64
Driscoll, Staff Sgt Edward J. Jnr 27
dry brushing 15, 32, 94–5

Early, Sgt Robert 105
Eisenhower, Dwight D. 42
El Guettar 49
Elrod, Maj. Henry Talmage 20
eye protection 11

Falaise Pocket 85
Filkosky, Sgt Robert 19
fillers 13
filters, applying 32–3, 36, 108
flesh & features, painting 22, 24, 40, 44
Fox Green Beach 70
Fredendall, Maj. Gen. Lloyd 42

Garand rifle 18, 43
Gavin, Col 59
General Motors 93
Germany, GIs in 112–14
glues 13, 99
Grenadier Regiment 725 70
Greyhound Armoured Car 114–17
Grumman Wildcat Fighters 19
Guadalcanal 18
gun barrel, brass 56

half-tracks 46–8, 59–65
  M2 64–5
  M3, M3A1 46–8, 49
  M15 anti-aircraft 59–63
Hayate (Japanese destroyer) 20
helmets
  A1 18

Brodie 18, 21
infantry 113–14
insignia on 113–14
Kelly 18
M1 18, 19, 45
tank crews' (M-1938) 66, 68
Hellcat (M18) 81, 86, 93–6
Higgins boats (LCVP) 26–7
Hiroshima 39
Howitzer, M1, M2, M7 ('Priest') 57
M2A1 57–8

Infantry 18, 39–41, 70, 73, 112–14
1st Division ('Big Red One') 70, 73
7th Division 39–41
29th Division 70, 73
Italy & Sicily 59–68
Iwo Jima, Battle of 19

Jackson Tank Destroyer 81, 104, 110–14
Jeep, Willys 97–9

Kasserine Pass 52
Kisaragi (Japanese destroyer) 20
knives, craft 12

landing vehicle, tracked (LVT) 18, 26–7, 30–4
Lee medium tank M3 52–4
Leiper, Lt Edwin 93
lighting 11
The Longest Day (film) 70
Ludendorff Bridge 102
Lunéville 93

M1 Abrams 104
M2 half-track 64–5, 120
M2A1 (Howitzer) 57–8
M3 GMC 49–51
M3 Gun Motor Carriage 49
M3 Lee medium tank 52–4
M3, M3A1 46–8
M4 18, 26, 27, 35–8, 57, 102
Thunderbolt IV 81–2
M5 59
M6 49
M8 Armoured Car 'Greyhound' 114–17
M10, M10A1 Tank Destroyers 80–1, 103
M15 anti-aircraft 59–63
M18 Hellcat 81, 86, 93–6
M1897A4 gun 49
M26 Pershing Heavy 103–9
M36 Jackson Tank Destroyer 81, 104, 110–14
Makin Atoll 27
Manteuffel, Gen. Hasso von 93
Marines 18–29
1st Corps Tank battalion 18, 26
1st Defense Battalion 19
2nd Division 27
1st and 6th Divisions 39
Marvin, Lee 19
masks 11
mine detection 77
Moselle, river 93

Nagasaki 39
National Museum of the Marine Corps (NMMC) 19
Normandy 69–84
North Africa, Torch Landings 42–58

Okinawa, Battle of 18, 39–41
Omaha Beach 69–70
Operation *Cobra* 72
Operation *Galvanic* 26–7
Operation *Husky* 59
Operation *Iceberg* 39
Operation *Market Garden* 9, 85–8, 97
Operation *Neptune* 69–84
Operation *Shoestring* 18
Operation *Watchtower* 18
optivisor 11
Orne Basin, Normandy 69

Pacific 18–41
paint 14–15
paintbrushes 15
painting tips 25, 28
larger figures 40
Panzer Brigade 113 93, 104
Panzerfaust 71
Parachute Regimental Combat Team, 505th 59
paratroopers 59, 69, 77–80, 88–90
Patton, Maj. Gen. George S. Jnr 42, 59, 85, 87, 93, 100–1
Pearl Harbor 18
Pershing M26 Heavy Tank 102–9
Philippines 49
pilots 23–5
pin washing 31–2, 35, 36, 108, 116

plasticard 12
Pointe du Hoc 70
polystyrene cement 13, 39, 99
power tools 12, 30, 64
preparation 11
Purple Heart 46
Putnam, Maj. Paul 19
putties 13
PVA 13, 78, 120

R35s (Vichy French) 46, 55
Ranger Battalions 59, 70
Remagen 102, 104
research 9
Ridgway, Maj. Gen. Matthew 59
Ripley's Believe it or Not Museum 19
Rudder, Lt Col James 70
Ryukyu Islands 39

safety 11
Sasebo Special Naval Landing Force 27
Satterlee, USS 70
Saving Private Ryan (film) 73, 74
scale 17
Sherman tanks
  M4 18, 26, 27, 35–8, 57, 102
  Cobra King 91–2
  Jumbo (M4A3E2) 91–2
  Thunderbolt IV 81–2
Shibazaki, Rear Admiral Kenji 27
shoulder flashes 73
Sicily & Italy 59–68
Smith, Maj. Julian C. 27
soft plastic, working with 118–120
Springfield rifle 18
Stuart (M3A1) light tank ('Honey') 55–6
Stuart, Gen. J.E.B. 55
superglue see cyanoacrylate

Talybont, HMS 70
tank crews 66–8
Tank Destroyer Battalions
  601st 49
  704th 93
tank destroyers 49–51, 80–1, 93, 103, 104, 110–14
tanks 18, 26, 27, 35–8, 46–8, 52–4, 55–6, 72, 81–2, 91–6, 102–9 *and see under individual names*
Tarawa, Battle of 18, 26–7, 28–38
Tenth Army 39
terrain 16
thinner 14, 15
Thunderbolt IV 81–2
Torch Landings, North Africa 42–58
tracks & running gear, assembling 105–6
tweezers 12

uniforms 18, 26
  camouflage 18, 26, 27
  differences 9
  infantry 39, 42–3, 72–80
  paratroopers 77, 88
  Rangers 72, 74–6
  tank crews 66–8
Utah Beach 69–70

vegetation 16–17
vehicle markings 9
ventilation 11
vices 12–13
Vichy French forces 42, 46, 55

Wake Island, Battle of 18, 19–26
wargames, fast painting for 88–90
weathering 15, 37–8, 96, 122
White Motor Company 46, 64
wire cutters 12
work area 11

Yarborough, Capt. William P. 77

Other Titles in the Series

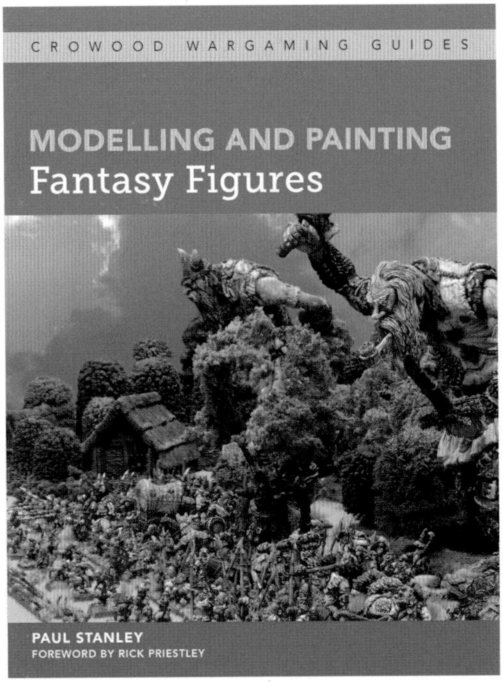

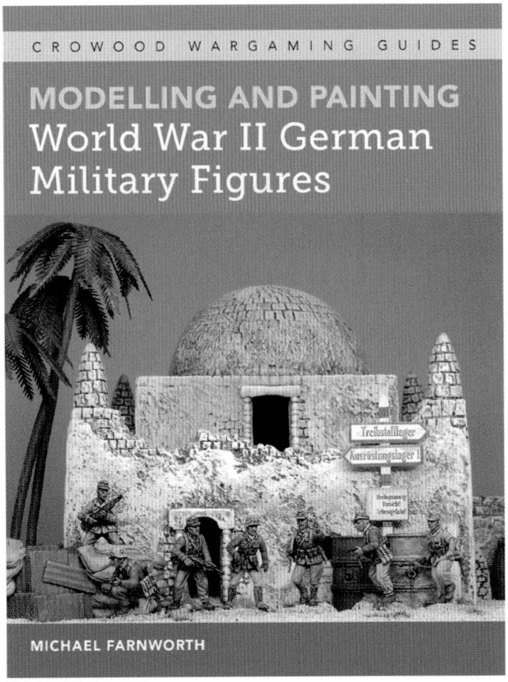

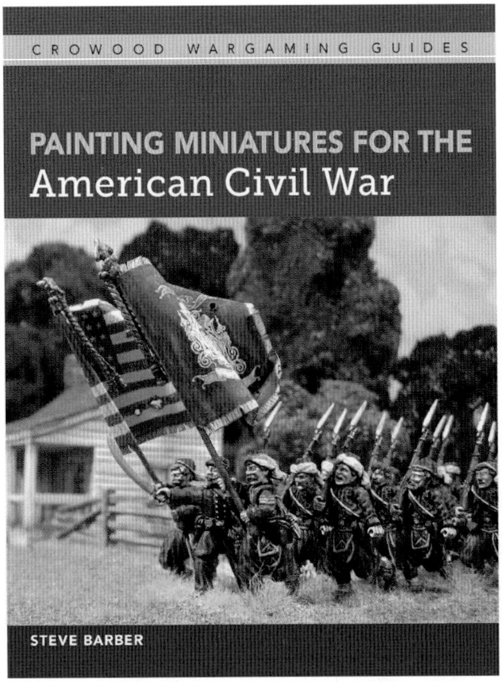

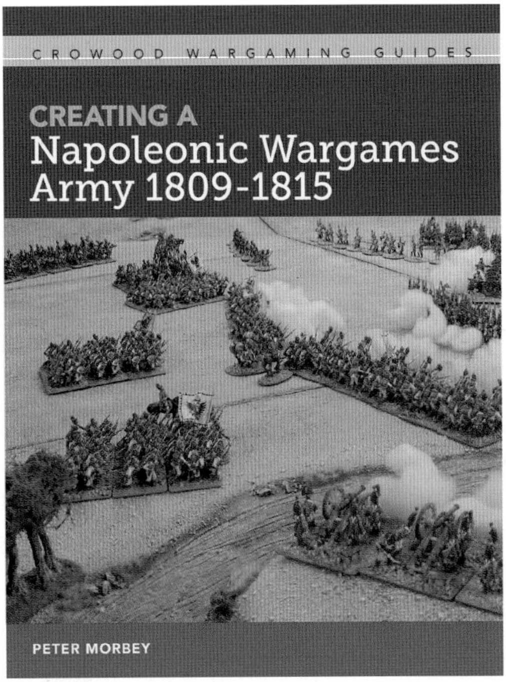